THE National ⚾ Pastime
A REVIEW OF BASEBALL HISTORY

TNP

If time is a river, just where are we now as we float with the current? Where have we been? Where may we be going on this journey?

I thought it would be fun to take readings of our position by looking at where our game, and by extension, our country, and our world were one, two, three, and more generations ago.

Mark Twain once wrote that biography is a matter of placing lamps at intervals along a person's life. He meant that no biographer can completely illuminate the entire story. But if we use his metaphor and place lamps at 25-year intervals in the biography of baseball, we can perhaps more dramatically see our progress, which we sometimes lose sight of in a day-by-day or year-by-year narrative history. We can see the game (and the world) as mom and dad saw it in 1961, as our grandparents saw it in 1941, our great grandparents in 1916, and so on back to 1841.

Fifty years from now some of our SABR members of today will write the history of 1991, as they look back from the vantage point of 2041. How will we and our world look to their grandchildren, who will read those histories? What stories will they cover—Rickey Henderson and Nolan Ryan? Jose Canseco and Cecil Fielder? The Twins and the Braves? Toronto's 4 million fans? What things do we take for granted that they will find quaint? What kind of game will the fans of that future world be seeing? What kind of world, beyond sports, will they live in?

It's to today's young people, the historians of tomorrow, and to their children and grandchildren that we dedicate this issue—from the SABR members of 1991 to the SABR members of 2041—with prayers that you will read it in a world filled with excitement and peace, where all your battles will be for pennants.

—JOHN B. HOLWAY

Editor: John B. Holway

THE NATIONAL PASTIME (ISSN 0734-6905, ISBN 0-910137-46-3), Number 11. Published by The Society for American Baseball Research, Inc., P.O. Box 93183, Cleveland, OH 44101. Postage paid at Birmingham, AL. Copyright 1992, The Society for American Baseball Research, Inc. All rights reserved. Reproduction in whole or part without written permission is prohibited. Printed by EBSCO Media, Birmingham, AL.

D1315189

Almost, almost

The Year 2 A.D. (After Doubleday)

MARK ALVAREZ

Officially, baseball was two years old in 1841. Abner Doubleday had invented the game in the summer of 1839 in a pasture in Cooperstown, NY, a site now enshrined as Doubleday Field.

This official version of the game's history was sufficient to plant the Hall of Fame in upstate New York and the name Doubleday in the minds of most Americans. Today, though, it's a version to which few subscribe—although many pay it the respect due a top-notch legend.

Abner Doubleday was assigned his status as father of the game early in the twentieth century by the Mills Commission, which had been established by Albert Spalding to discover a purely American origin for baseball. That it came up with a general of the Civil War, a hero of both Sumter and Gettysburg, was a plum that the publicity-savvy Spalding couldn't resist plucking.

The evidence for the Doubleday story was a letter sent to the committee by one Abner Graves, a Colorado mining engineer who'd been raised in Cooperstown, and who claimed to be present on the day when the future general laid down the rules for the game that would become the national pastime.

The boys of Cooperstown were apparently playing a version of Two Old Cat, similar to the game familiar to many of us as work-up or scrub. Between twenty and fifty of the scholars at the Otsego Academy and Green's Select School participated at one time in these matches. The batter hit the ball, ran to a goal fifty feet away, and returned. If he made it, he stayed at bat. If someone caught his fly, the fielder came in to hit. The batter could also be put out by the old-fashioned expedient of being "plunked," as Graves put it, or hit by a thrown ball. The most interesting feature of the game Graves described is that the tosser stood close to the batter and

lofted the ball straight upward about six feet for the batsman to strike at on its fall. It sounds like a cross between slow-pitch softball and hitting fungoes.

Graves said that Doubleday improved this primitive game in several ways.

First, he made it a team game, with definite sides.

Second, he limited the number of players on each side to eleven (not nine), so as to avoid collisions and injuries.

Third, he established that there would be four bases, not just two goals. Graves claimed that Doubleday then named the game "Base Ball" after his new inventions.

Even casual students of the game now know that young Doubleday couldn't have joined the other boys in the pasture that day, because he was at West Point. But even if he'd been granted a pass for the specific purpose of developing a national pastime for his developing nation, the game he came up with wasn't baseball. It was simply a version of the town ball already being played everywhere in one form or another.

Actually such games had been played in America almost from the beginning of European settlement. A second wave of Pilgrims—"lusty yonge men, and wilde enough"—got into hot water for playing ball in Plymouth on Christmas Day, 1621. The game they played was stoolball, an old English pastime in which stools were used as rudimentary bases.

In its simplest form, one player stood in front of a stool and used his hand to swat the ball, while the thrower tried to slip it by him and bounce it off the little seat. Players kept score by counting the number of times the hitter made contact with the ball, and they changed places when the thrower hit his target. With more players and more furniture, players ran from stool to stool after a hit and could be put out if a fielder drilled them with the ball before they reached their goal. Any modern American seeing this form of the ancient

game in progress would recognize its resemblance, however distant, to baseball. And even if he didn't know that stools were once called *crickets*, any Englishman would notice that the upturned three-legged stool looks like the stumps that the batter guards in modern-day cricket. By setting up two stools this way, players would have created a primitive cricket pitch. It looks as if we've got what anthropologists call a common ancestor here—the primitive precursor of two great national sports.

The term "base ball" has been in use at least since the early eighteenth century, often used interchangeably with "round ball," "goal ball," "baste ball," "rounders," and "town ball." By the early nineteenth century, both cricket and town ball in its various forms were commonly played throughout the land. Cricket, with its highly developed rules, sophisticated skills, and multiday matches, was popular with more leisured classes, while American farmers and townspeople hacked away at their own more primitive games, which always featured "plunking," "soaking," or "burning" as a way to put the batter or runner out. In 1833 the Olympic Town Ball Club—overcoming a strong prejudice against grown men wasting their time at such nonsense—was founded in Philadelphia. But the sport was really centered in New England, where, in 1859, what is often called the first intercollegiate baseball game (Amherst 73, Williams 32) was really a match at town ball.

By the early 1840s, probably by the year 1841, young middle-class New Yorkers were beginning to meet on Manhattan fields to play ball among themselves. And during the season of 1845, something happened. Exactly what stars came into conjunction we'll probably never know. What we're sure of is this:

First, that by September 1845, a number of the regular ballplayers had formed a club.

Second, they called their new organization the Knickerbocker Base Ball Club, probably after a volunteer fire company a number of them belonged to.

And third, the Knickerbockers then published the first written rules of a game that was a distinct departure from the town ball games of the era. As their game, the new Knickerbockers settled on a sport that may seem a bit primitive to modern eyes, but is nonetheless recognizable as real baseball.

The final rule changes that moved those old-fashioned children's games over the line toward true baseball are often credited to Alexander Cartwright, who has a plaque in Cooperstown to show for it. But they were more likely the result of many Manhattan players—future Knickerbockers and non-Knickerbockers alike—reacting over a period of years to their own needs and circumstances. A broken nose on a Wall Street lawyer, for example, would be a sufficient reason to outlaw "plugging" and replace it with tagging and

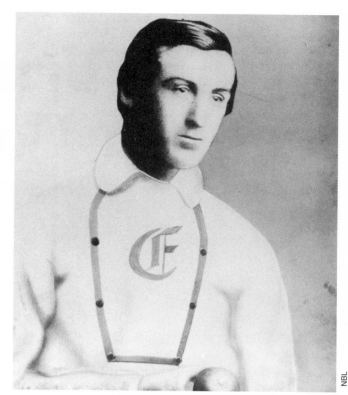

Jim Creighton, baseball's first fireballer

forceouts. And the casual nature of the games probably led to the choice of bases on the ground—easily represented by caps, bags, or articles of clothing, just as they are on sandlots today—over the old-fashioned posts of rounders and town ball, which would have to be especially carried to the field. Likewise, the move to establish foul territory (in most versions of town ball, as in cricket, there was none) might well have been a reaction to the fact that the Murray Hill playing site that these young men used was being reduced in size by construction of both commercial buildings and a railway cut. Under these urban conditions, the scope of play may have had to be concentrated and directed. It's ironic to think that baseball, which is often given rural, bucolic associations, may have been forced into its modern shape by the booming growth of our largest city and the uncomfortable proximity of a glue factory wall.

But in 1841, all this was still to come. Jim Creighton, the game's first great pitcher, would be born during this year, and so would Asa Brainard, the unbeatable hurler for Cincinnati's Red Stockings of 1869, but only two or three others destined to make big names for themselves in the game were yet alive. The year 1841 was late in baseball's centuries-long gestation period, but the game, like most of its players, had yet to be delivered.

The moment when baseball became our national pastime

The Turning Point

W. LLOYD JOHNSON

In March 1866 the future of baseball was uncertain. There were no King Kellys, Babe Ruths, or Bill Veecks to stimulate interest among the thousands of returning Civil War veterans. Yet by October 1866, baseball had reached a popularity from which there would be no turning back.

As Dr. Harold Seymour put it in *Baseball, The Early Years,* "Attendance records were shattered in 1866 when the membership of the National Association of Base Ball Players swelled to a grand total of 202 clubs from seventeen different states and the District of Columbia."

The warriors returned home to an indefinite future. After four years of sleeping on the ground, pillaging, sporadic meals, etc., the weary Union veterans found they had much in common with the Johnny Rebs—guns, suspicion, hardness, and baseball.

In Florence, Massachusetts, 6,000 fans saw the hometown Eagles defeat the Hampdens of Chicopee, 28–11, for the championship of Western Massachusetts.

In Washington, more than 7,000, including President Andrew Johnson, watched the Excelsiors defeat the Washington Nationals, 33–28.

In Philadelphia more than 12,000 spectators at 15th and Columbia Grounds watched the host Athletics drub the Washington Nationals, 22–6.

In Hoboken, New Jersey, 15,000 packed into the Elysian Fields, the "Home of Baseball"—the first game may have been played there in 1845—to watch the Brooklyn Atlantics snatch a come-from-behind victory over the New York Mutuals, 17–15.

Then came the Championship Match Games between the Atlantics and the Athletics.

The Athletics had one avowed professional on the roster, second baseman Al Reach, who went on to found the sport-

ing goods company. A rival manager, Harry Wright, charged that two other A's were also getting paid under the table. These may have been third baseman Lipman Pike and pitcher Dickey McBride, a world class cricket bowler. (Eleven years later the Athletics converted to a cricket club and went on to win the world championship over an astonished English team.)

The Atlantics starred Little Dickie Pearce, the inventor of the bunt, at shortstop. "Old Reliable" Joe Start was considered the best first baseman until Cap Anson and probably should be in the Hall of Fame. Brooklyn also boasted outfielders Bob Ferguson and John Chapman, who shared the eponymous nickname, "Death to Flying Things." Second baseman Sam Crane went on to fame as a sports writer and confidant of John McGraw, and pitcher Al Pratt would help found the American Association in 1882.

On the morning of the first "Grand Match" in Philadelphia, scorecards were printed and sold for the first time. All 8,000 twenty-five-cent tickets were sold, and as much as $5 was paid for chairs or benches. Treetops, fences, and elevated stations were dense with people, yet coaches and wagons continued to bring more excited spectators. "There could not have been less than 30,000 present in and around the grounds," wrote one newspaper, "the contest being conceded to be the most important ever played in the country."

By almost superhuman effort a small space was cleared and the game commenced "with the hope that the appearance of the players in the field would cause the assemblage to fall back . The Athletics batted first and scored two runs. The Atlantics came to bat and had one out, two men on base and the fourth "striker" up, when "the swelling and surging forward of the assemblage rendered it impossible to proceed further." The game was then called, and there followed a

scene of "majestic confusion," as the crowd "flowed into the field from all sides and covered the entire grounds."

The game was rescheduled for October 15 at Capitoline Grounds in Brooklyn before 19,000 persons. Temporary planking formed rude bleacher seats, while two small, roofed amphitheaters served the ladies. Many people preferred to stand on the surrounding hillocks, every available seat having been filled since early morning. Despite the general drabness of nineteenth century clothing, color splashes competed with the autumnal colors of nearby foliage. The blue-trousered teams were distinguishable by their cap colors, blue for the Atlantics and red for the Athletics. There was no mistaking the smells of the food vendors. Hard cider, beer full of sediment, sandwiches gathered from "unreliable sources," and what were described as "jonilized" cakes (possibly "johnny cakes") stuffed the patrons.

The painting, "The Second Great Match Game for the Championship, 1866," which hangs in the Hall of Fame, shows the faces of real Brooklyn aldermen and actual portraits of the players, as well as pickpockets and poolsellers.

The contest was close until the Atlantics scored eight runs in the seventh inning, leading to a 27–17 victory.

Seven days later came the rematch. Twenty thousand people crowded into Philadelphia to watch the Athletics best the Atlantics, 31–12. Disputes over the distribution of gate receipts led to cancellation of any more games, and the Atlantics claimed the mythical National Championship.

More than 68,000 ball fans had attended the three games. On those bright autumn days of 1866, baseball became entrenched as our national pastime.

An archaeologist asks—

Where was the Jefferson Street Grounds?

Exactly where was Philadelphia's Jefferson Street Grounds, site of "the great game for the Championship of the United States" that Lloyd Johnson writes about above (and ten years later site of the first major league game)?

Most references say the park was situated at 25th and Jefferson Streets. As an "urban archeologist," I believe the old books are in error and transposed two numerals, so that the real location was *52nd* and Jefferson.

I began my search by taking a ride to 25th and Jefferson in North Philadelphia. What an unusual place to play baseball, I thought, far from the main area of activity in Philadelphia at that time. How did 30,000 fans get there?

I went to the library, and in an 1870 map of the city I found nothing that could be a ballpark anywhere in North Philadelphia.

But in a 1900 map book, I checked the 44th and Parkside site in South Philadelphia, where the Negro league Philadelphia Stars later played. On the same page, at 52nd St. and Jefferson, was an area marked "Athletic Grounds." It is only two blocks from the site of the 1876 Centennial exhibition, a world attraction that year. It is also diagonally across from 51st and Columbia Avenue. (One authority claims the site was at *15th* and Columbia.)

I believe this may be the real site of the historic baseball field.

Since nothing has been built there in more than a century except for some railroad tracks, I plan to make some archeological digs on the site to see just what I can dig up.

— *JOEL SPIVAK*

We're shocked. Shocked!

Boss Tweed and the Mutuals

DAVID Q. VOIGT

William Marcy "Boss" Tweed was one of the most corrupt political bosses who surfaced in American cities after the Civil War. As the chief power in New York's Tammany Hall, Tweed's ring turned the one-time social club into a major force in city politics. By controlling Democratic Party nominations and the patronage system, Tweed made a fortune from graft and reportedly defrauded the city of an estimate $30 million.

Among Tweed's machinations was his control of the New York Mutual Base Ball Club. The team's president was also the city coroner, and in 1865 Boss Tweed had helped elevate that worthy to a high post in the National Association of Base Ball Players.

Charges of game-fixing surrounded the Mutuals, but there was only one *documented* case. In 1865 three players— Tom Devyr, Ed Duffy, and William Wansley—had divided a $100 bribe offer from gamblers for throwing a game to the Brooklyn Eckfords. Following an investigation, all three were expelled, but by 1870 all were reinstated.

The Mutuals the year before they got caught. Wansley is standing seventh from the left, Devyr eleventh.

RUCKER

Boston's final, formidable AA club

The Red Stockings' Last Hurrah

ROBERT L. TIEMANN

As pennant winners in their only season, the American Association Boston Reds set a record that will probably never be broken. Because of the "war" between the Association and the National League, this outstanding team did not get to test its mettle in a World Series. And because the AA folded after the season, it never got a chance to repeat.

And they won their title despite major injuries to two key players and the defection of one of baseball's biggest stars.

In 1890, the Boston Players' League club had won the pennant and brought in more money than any other club in baseball. After the merger of several National League and Players' League clubs had killed the Brotherhood, the Boston PL owners, Charles A. Prince and Julian B. Hart, refused to quit. The AA offered them a franchise, and in the uneasy months of peace that winter, the NL acquiesced, though the owners made it clear that they were not at all happy.

Undeterred, Prince and Hart began signing players for their new team, dubbed the Reds, or Red Stockings, which would play in the former Players' League grounds on Congress Street, with its chummy fences—just 250 feet to left and under 300 to right.

Their roster was filled with former PL players.

Michael "King" Kelly, manager of the Boston PL champs, was the most prominent, but when war broke out with the NL in the spring, the AA decided to place Kelly at the head of its new Cincinnati team.

Even without the King, the Boston Reds were a formidable bunch.

At first base was Dan Brouthers (pronounced "Broothers"), one of the great sluggers of the nineteenth century. Then thirty-three years old, the strapping 207-pounder had already won three batting titles and had hit .330 with the Boston Players League the year before.

Left fielder Hardy Richardson, also from the Boston Players, had hit .326 in 1890 and led the league in RBIs with 143.

A righthanded swinger, he could reach the left field wall.

Another Boston alumni, speedy Englishman Tommy Brown, thirty-one, was a .276-hitting leadoff man.

The rest of the infielders were third baseman Bill Joyce, .252; second baseman John "Cub" Stricker, .244; and Paul Radford, a converted outfielder at short, .292.

The youngsters on the team were little outfielder and captain Hugh Duffy, .320, and a big catcher, Charlie "Duke" Farrell, .290. Both were New England Irishmen and both came from the Chicago club. Farrell had hit only 2 homers in '90.

The pitching staff was led by Charlie Buffinton, a paunchy righthander from Massachusetts with a 19–15 record for Philadelphia in 1890; George Haddock, who had a 9–26 record with last-place Buffalo, and Darby O'Brien, who went 8–16 with Cleveland.

Unfortunately, the Reds could field their best lineup for only six games all season. Richardson broke his foot sliding home on a homer on April 30 and would be out for two and a half months. Manager Art Irwin moved Farrell to left field.

Defending champion Louisville got out of the gate fastest, winning twelve of its first sixteen, but with pitching ace Scott Stratton out with a sore shoulder, the Colonels were soon struggling to stay out of last place.

The Baltimore Orioles took a brief turn in the lead, but their weak infield kept them from staying up with the leaders. The Orioles had to use lefthanded captain George Van Haltren at shortstop much of the first half before finally acquiring a rookie from Cedar Rapids named John McGraw.

The Reds held the lead for most of May.

Then came a strong challenge from the St. Louis Browns. Outfielders Tip O'Neill, Tommy McCarthy, and Dummy Hoy hit .321, .310, and .291 that year, respectively. Third baseman Denny Lyons hit .315 with 11 homers. Workhorse pitcher Jack Stivetts posted a 33–22 record, and little lefty

Will McGill went 19–10 after coming over from Cincinnati.

On June 16 they had won eleven of their last twelve games, and they knocked the Reds out of first place by winning a ten-inning thriller, 11–10. The next day the largest crowd of the season, 17,439, jammed Sportsman's Park and saw Boston retake the lead by winning, 6–5. Duffy got the Reds their first run with a bunt that scored Brown, and home runs by Farrell and Murphy gave Buffinton enough to withstand a mammoth homer in the ninth by Lyons. In the rubber game Haddock was knocked out of the box in the third inning but the Red Stockings rallied to win, 8–6.

On July 2 the Reds received another blow when scrappy Bill Joyce, batting .309, broke his leg sliding. Bill had scored 76 runs in 65 games and would be hard to replace. Irwin transferred Farrell to the hot corner, and the Duke responded magnificently, playing steady defense and developing into the top clutch hitter in the circuit.

The Reds and Browns seesawed with the lead until their next meeting at Boston in early July. This time St. Louis won the first two games, coming from behind both times, to take over first place on July 8. But in the final game of the series on July 10, Farrell connected for a three-run homer to give the Reds a 5–2 win and the league lead again.

This time they would not be headed. Richardson returned to left field a week later. And St. Louis owner Chris Von der Ahe made a critical mistake by releasing rookie pitcher Clark Griffith. Boston signed the youngster August 3, and he became the fourth man on the Reds' staff while the Browns suffered from a lack of pitching depth.

Meanwhile, Cincinnati was in financial trouble all summer and folded August 16. Kelly returned to Boston. His debut on August 19 drew 11,056 fans, and his first Saturday outing attracted 11,287—the two biggest Boston crowds of the season.

But after only four games Kelly jumped across town to the National League Beaneaters for a record $25,000. He played only 16 games for them, but the deal effectively ruined the peace talks between the leagues.

The Reds didn't miss the King, however. They led the league in batting, slugging, on base percentage, hits, runs, and steals. Brouthers batted a league-leading .350, Duffy .336, Brown .321, and Farrell .302. The Duke, playing four positions (catcher, outfield, third, and first), led the league in homers with 12, and RBIs with 110. Duffy and Brouthers were close behind in RBIs with 108, and the fleet-footed Brown scored 177 times.

The pitchers also had fine years. Griffith was 3–1, O'Brien 18–13, Buffinton 29–9, and Haddock made a complete turnaround at 34–11.

The Reds won the pennant with ease.

They had been negotiating with the Chicago Colts, NL leaders, for a World series. But a late eighteen-game winning streak by the Beaneaters snatched the NL pennant for Boston. The Reds issued a challenge to the Beaneaters, but were met with stony silence. Too bad. This would have been history's only all-Boston World Series.

The Beaneaters would probably have been favored to win on the strength of better pitching, but the Reds' pitchers, especially Buffinton and Haddock, were capable of holding their own even against their rivals' aces, John Clarkson (33–19) and Kid Nichols (30–17). And the Reds' offense was probably a little stronger than the Beaneaters', although one wonders how righthanded sluggers Harry Stovey (16 homers) and Billy Nash (95 RBIs) might have done in tiny Congress Park.

We will never know which Boston team would have won. And we will never know if the Reds could have continued to dominate the AA; they were bought out in the merger agreement before the next season began. The Beaneaters paid a heavy price to eliminate their rivals, and baseball history suffered as well.

What happened to the Reds players? They dispersed.

Only Duffy stayed in Boston, helping the Beaneaters to six pennants in seven years. In 1894 he would hit .440, a record that still stands.

Richardson went to Washington, where he hit .200 and was released in a month to sign with New York for a final season. Farrell went to Pittsburgh, where he batted .215.

Brouthers and Haddock moved to Brooklyn. Dan won his fifth batting championship and led the league in hits and RBIs. George also had another fine year at 29–13.

Buffinton was only 3–8 at Baltimore before getting his release in July, his final year in the majors.

Griffith spent two years in the minors, but he had six straight twenty-win seasons in the NL after that.

O'Brien never pitched another game. He died in 1892 at the age of twenty-four.

Charlie Buffinton, in sleeker days.

In the aftermath of the Brotherhood Rebellion

The Magnates Regain Control

BOB GELZHEISER

Historians and true believers have long argued that baseball is a reflection of American society. Babe Ruth is the perfect symbol of the Roaring Twenties, and Jackie Robinson is synonymous with the Civil Rights movement.

During the last decades of the nineteenth century, professional baseball was a microcosm of much of what was happening in American business. During what Mark Twain called the "Gilded Age," a new industrial order was emerging. Corporate leaders believed that regulation and control of all aspects of their industry were the keys to success. Competition had to be absorbed or destroyed to prevent market forces from determining prices and limiting profits.

The baseball industry embraced this mode of thinking, and throughout the 1880s regulated markets, labor, ticket prices, and wages, so much so that even Andrew Carnegie would have been proud.

For most of the 1880s, the nation had two major leagues: the American Association and the National League. In 1891, disagreements between these leagues fractured the monopoly and unleashed market forces on the baseball industry, thus making that year a peculiar one for the business of baseball.

The backbone of the baseball monopoly was the National Agreement, first implemented in 1883. Boundaries of teams were sacrosanct, which eliminated competition. Teams could reserve a specified number of players, and these were bound to their teams indefinitely. This kept wages artificially low and enabled organizations to sell players for substantial sums. Member teams agreed to honor each other's black-lists, suspensions, and expulsions. Disputes between teams, or players and teams, were submitted to a six-man Board of Arbitration made up of club representatives. Players weren't represented on the board, and its decisions were final.

The National League, under the leadership of capitalists such as Albert Spalding, implemented many additional regulations. Ticket prices were set at fifty cents, the sale of alcohol and Sunday games were forbidden, and player behavior on and off the field was rigidly regulated, at least in theory. These policies proved to be successful as the game's popularity and profitability boomed in the 1880s.

The established order was threatened in 1890. Angered at arbitrary player sales, a short-lived salary classification plan, and a general affront to their "manliness," National League

Albert G. Spalding, magnate of magnates.

players united with capitalists less obsessed with control and formed the Players League. For many baseball magnates, this was their worst nightmare come true. Not only did the League give players a degree of control, but it also created free market competition, something the National League had fought for most of its history to eliminate.

Unfortunately for the players, the 1890 season was disastrous. Many cities had more than one team, the quality of play was reduced, and by midseason most fans had grown apathetic and stopped attending games; consequently, most teams in the nation's three major leagues lost money. After the season, Spalding helped to orchestrate a consolidation that terminated the Players League but allowed many of its owners to merge their clubs and capital with American Association and National League franchises. A new, stricter, National Agreement was implemented, and a National Board consisting of one representative from each of the National League and Western and American Associations was established that had the final say in most disputes. Spalding and his fellow magnates believed that they had reestablished the baseball monopoly.

The peace between the National League and American Association did not last long. The National Board had been given the responsibility of dividing up the surplus players that resulted from consolidation. Most American Association franchises believed that each of the major leagues would be allowed to reserve fourteen players who had been on a team's roster in 1889 or 1890, and the remaining players would be distributed to National Agreement teams by the Board depending on a franchise's needs. Association owners were angered when the Board allowed Pittsburgh and Boston of the National League to sign Louis Bierbauer and Harry Stovey, respectively, both of whom had jumped to the Players League in 1890 but had played for the Association's Philadelphia Athletics in 1889. The Association protested the ruling, but the National Board, citing a technicality, ruled that the players would remain the property of their new National League teams.

American Association clubs were further incensed when many National League teams reserved as many as twenty-five players in an era when most team rosters consisted of only thirteen or fourteen men. These teams then sold, traded, or released these players. The American Association believed that the National League was concerned only with its own interests and could not be trusted. Consequently it dropped out of the National Agreement in February 1891.

The year 1891 was hectic for players and owners. The courts ruled that since the Association was not a member of the Agreement, the reserve clause did not regulate the movement of players between National League teams and the Association. This free market did not benefit the American Association. The National League had emerged from the confrontation with the Players League as the strongest league in the nation. Several Players League franchises had merged with National League teams, and generally organizations in the senior league were better capitalized.

The American Association believed that money would not be the only factor that determined where players chose to play. Its owners claimed that they treated players as "gentlemen" while their rival viewed them as "slaves" and "brutes." They believed that the players, smarting from their bitter defeat of 1890 and still craving respect, would flock to the American Association.

They were wrong. Most players proved to have short memories, and went to the team that offered them the most money, regardless of which league it was in.

Perhaps the most serious problem that the American Association faced was that the tremendous capital and revenue differential among its teams, which reduced the competitive balance. Boston, which had played in the Players League in 1890, had the resources to attract new stars and to retain its former Players League standouts: Dan Brouthers, Tom Brown, and Hardy Richardson. It won the American Association pennant in 1891. Second-place St. Louis had played in the American Association in 1890, was able to keep stars Tommy McCarthy and Jack Stivetts and lure other fine players.

These teams dominated the National League in 1891, and most of their competition was out of the pennant race by midsummer. (The third-place Baltimore and Philadelphia teams finished twenty-two games off the pace.)

This lack of competition, plus poor weather in some cities, helped to keep attendance low despite the American Association's twenty-five cent admission price, which was half of what the National League charged.

The Association attempted to reduce the disparity between rich and poor teams by evenly dividing gate receipts between the home and visiting clubs for all games except those played on holidays. On holidays the Association's receipts were to be divided equally among all teams. However, these revenue-sharing measures failed to keep most AA teams in the black, and by the season's end, most clubs were near bankruptcy.

The Association had hoped to gain additional revenue by playing a postseason "World Series" against the National League's best club, but its rival circuit refused to meet in such a match.

The American Association folded after the 1891 season. Four of its franchises—Baltimore, St. Louis, Washington, and Louisville—were purchased by the National League for $130,000.00. Spalding rejoiced at the demise of his rival. He claimed that this would lead to a "permanent peace and prosperity." The peace, such as it was, lasted a decade. The prosperity never materialized. The "Big League" was unwieldy, the country was ravaged by depression, and many clubs lost money throughout the "gay '90s."

The finest black team of the 19th century lost a daring experiment to integrate the game

The Cubans' Last Stand

JERRY MALLOY

"There are players among these colored men that are equal to any white players on the ballfield. If you don't think so, go out and see the Cuban Giants play. This club, with its strongest players on the field, would play a favorable game against such clubs as the New Yorks or Chicagos."
—The Sporting News, 1887

Neither Cubans nor giants, from 1885–1890 the Cuban Giants boasted, from time to time, such stars as second baseman Frank Grant and pitcher George Washington Stovey, respectively the best black player and the best black pitcher of the 19th century.

The club was formed in 1885, just a year after Moses Fleetwood Walker had become the first Negro in the major leagues (with Toledo of the American Association).

The Cubans were probably not, as black historian Sol White reported, made up of Long Island waiters speaking a gibberish "Spanish."

Their owner was Walter Cook, scion of a wealthy Trenton family, who raised many an eyebrow in upper social circles by inviting his players to his home as guests. Manager S.K. Govern was a native of the West Indies.

In their first year the Cuban Giants felt cocky enough to take on two white major league clubs. The seventh-place New York Metropolitans of the American Association, starring Dave Orr (.342), beat them 11–3, and the fourth-place Philadelphia Athletics of the same league, with home run champ Harry Stovey, defeated them, 13–7.

In 1886 the Cubans' star pitcher, George Washington Stovey, the light-skinned Canadian lefty, was literally kidnapped from them by Jersey City of the Eastern (International) League. He was spirited away at night to pitch against Newark in a crucial series in a game he won, 1–0. He also struck out 22 men in one game against Bridgeport. In all, Stovey was 16–15 with Jersey City, with a 1.13 ERA.

The New York Giants tried to buy Stovey to pitch a big series against Cap Anson's Chicagos. Stovey had his bags all packed to leave for the ballpark before the deal was called off—Anson had already refused to play against Fleet Walker in an 1883 exhibition.

Meanwhile, even without Stovey, the Giants ran up a 35-game winning streak. Their victims included Cincinnati, fifth in the American Association, with second baseman Bid McPhee and pitcher Tony Mullane (33–27), and the Kansas City Cowboys, who finished seventh in the National League. Finally, Charlie Comiskey's AA champion St. Louis Browns, starring Tip O'Neill (.335) and Dave Foutz (41–16), beat them, 9–3.

Their closest black rivals, the New York Gorhams, were no opposition; the Cubans trounced them, 25–4.

The Cubans were "the happiest set of men in the world," Sol White wrote. At salaries of $12–18 a week, "not one would have changed his position with the President of the United States."

In 1887 Stovey moved to Newark, where he and Fleet Walker formed the first black battery in organized ball, the so-called "Spanish battery." The New York Mets wanted to buy them, but Anson (again) reportedly stomped off the field in April rather than play against them, effectively ending hopes of opening the major leagues to Negroes.

Thus rejected, Stovey stayed in Newark and compiled a 34–14 record.

Meanwhile, after wintering in Florida, Govern's team defeated two International League clubs—Syracuse, 6–4,

and Newark, 14–1 and 8–2. It is not known whether Stovey pitched either of the Newark games.

The Cubans also beat Indianapolis, last in the National League, and Cincinnati, second in the Association.

Then they met Detroit, the National League pennant winners, starring batting champ Sam Thompson (.372, 166 RBI), Dan Brouthers (.338), Hardy Richardson (.328), and Deacon White (.303). Cubans hurler Billy Whyte was winning, 4–2, after seven innings, when errors lost the game, 6–4.

Several thousand persons in West Farms, New York came to see the Cubes face the Browns, who repeated as AA champions, with batting and home run champ Tip O'Neill (.435), Comiskey (.335), pitcher Silver King (34–11), and others. However, every Brown except Comiskey and one other refused to play them.

But the Cubans remained popular with their fans. At season's end, the Cubes were handed bouquets "as a token of appreciation of the people of New York for your good ball playing and gentlemanly conduct."

By 1888 the Giants were performing before large crowds at New York's 14th Street Ferry Grounds, and the New York *Sun* called them "one of the best teams in the city."

At year's end Govern issued a call for a "championship of races"—his Cuban Giants against other ethnic all star teams of Irish, English, Spanish, etc. It would be his "negro team against the world," Govern said. However, no one responded to his call.

In 1889, the Cubans scored their biggest coup: They signed both Stovey and little infielder Frank Grant, the Joe Morgan of his day. In three years in Buffalo of the International League Grant had batted .344, .353, and .356 and had led the league in homers once.

But some of his teammates raised a ruckus over having their pictures taken with him. When he demanded $250 a month for 1889, the rest of the team rebelled. *The Sporting News* reported that "the boys acknowledge that he is a good player, but ... their sentiment is that colored men should not play with white men."

Gratefully, the Cuban Giants welcomed him and embarked on a daring experiment: They entered the all-white Middle States League, representing Trenton.

Strangely, Stovey was ineffective, with only a 1–4 record. But Grant batted .313 as the Cubes fought Harrisburg for the pennant. They had apparently won a close race until the league threw out several of their victories to give the flag to Harrisburg.

The next year, 1890, Harrisburg stole Grant away, while York stole most of the rest of the Cubans, and Stovey deserted them all to pitch for Troy, New York. Grant hit .333, but the league folded when Harrisburg deserted it.

In 1891 the Cubans tried one more time to play alongside whites. With both Stovey and Grant back, plus the young infielder, Sol White, they entered the Connecticut State League, representing Ansonia.

The season opened inauspiciously for Stovey, who was arrested for assaulting an elderly woman in Hoosick Falls,

The great Frank Grant

New York. The case was later dismissed.

(A month earlier, Fleet Walker had stabbed to death an ex-con who "made a bad move when he came for me." The jury acquitted Walker in a verdict received with "a tremendous roar of cheers.")

The Cubans played only three games in the league before it also folded. Bad weather and shaky finances were blamed, but the Cubans themselves deserved part of the blame for ignoring scheduled league games to barnstorm.

For all intents and purposes, baseball's Color Curtain had closed in 1891, not to be parted again for another 55 years. (One more feeble attempt at integration was made in 1896, when the Acme Colored Giants joined the obscure Oil and Iron League.)

The Gorhams, now managed by Govern, grabbed Stovey, Grant, and White and proclaimed themselves the "Big Gorhams"—White would later call them the best black team of the century. Even President Benjamin Harrison came out to watch them play.

The Gorhams did not survive the depression of the '90s. But the Cubans did survive and endured into the 20th century as the "Genuine Cuban Giants" and the off-shoot "Cuban X-Giants."

In 1909 Grant, White, and some of the other old Cuban Giants got together one more time for an old-timers' game to benefit black pioneer Bud Fowler. Only one of them, Sol White, would live until 1947 to see Jackie Robinson trot onto the field as a member of the Brooklyn Dodgers.

A Mammoth Homer and A Perfect Game

ROBERT L. TIEMANN

After the collapse of the Players League, Charlie Comiskey, Tip O'Neill, and some of the other old Browns came back to St. Louis for the final year of the dying American Association.

A battle for first place against the Boston Reds attracted a record crowd of over 17,000 on June 7. The Reds won despite a mammoth home run by St. Louis third baseman Denny Lyons (11 homers, .315).

Lyons was prone to drunkenness, and he and several players had had run-ins with owner Chris Von Der Ahe. Just before the end of the 1891 season Tommy McCarthy (.310) and Jack Stivetts (33–22) signed with the National League for 1892. After the end of the campaign, the exodus from St. Louis became general.

The only player Chris was able to retain was hometown pitcher Ted Breitenstein, who had been farmed to Grand Rapids for most of the year before finally getting to start the final day of the season. He responded with a no-hitter, facing the minimum 27 batters, in beating eighth-place Louisville.

Denny Lyons, reaching for one in Philadelphia

Dapper Ted Breitenstein

enth with a single and dashed to third when Heinie Zimmerman (.291) hit a ground single to right. Cy Williams (.279), the league leader in homers, knocked in the only run with an infield out. Pete won, 2–1.

Again in the seventh Brooklyn got a runner to third with one out, but Alexander fanned Smith and Myers to put out the flame for the fourth time.

He hurled 16 shutouts. He might have had 24.

June 3. More cardiac arrest at Baker Bowl. The Cardinals' Bob Bescher (.235) opened the game with a double and was sacrificed to third, before the Nebraskan struck out the third and fourth hitters, Dots Miller (.238) and Rogers Hornsby (.313).

In the fifth, with the Phillies ahead, 1–0, St. Louis loaded the bases with no outs. Alex got a ground forceout at home on Lee Meadows, but Bescher sent a deep fly to left. Possum Whitted made the catch and made what the Philadelphia writers termed the best throw of his Quaker City career. It sailed on a fly to Killefer, who easily made the putout.

The Cards' first batter in the seventh reached second on a single and error. Bruno Betzel (.233) lashed a liner over second, but Bert Niehoff made an over-the-head catch with his back to the plate and doubled the runner at second. Moments later a running, leaping catch by center fielder Dode Paskert off the bat of Frank Snyder (.259) saved a game-tying home run.

July 7 The Cardinals got just one runner to third base, but Pete proceeded to strike out Roy Corhan (.210) and induce Meadows to tap weakly to the mound.

Paskert in center had to make several breathtaking catches, two off the bat of Bescher. The most heroic was his sixth-inning running catch of a home run drive ticketed for the clubhouse gates.

August 2 The Cubs squandered several scoring opportunities with less than two outs.

In the fifth, they put men on second and third with no outs. But Alex bore down and got Chuck Wortman (.201) to pop to shortstop, fanning Art Wilson (.227) and inducing Prendergast to hit back to the box.

In the sixth, with a man on second and one out, Mann laced a screamer which Niehoff snared and threw to Bancroft for a double play.

Leading off the twelfth, Zimmerman took second on Bancroft's wild throw. But Dave redeemed himself on the next play when he caught Joe Kelly's rifle-shot grounder and caught Zimmerman in a rundown, Kelly taking second. Two intentional walks loaded the bases with two out, and Alex faced his counterpart, Prendergast. He struck him out.

The Phils won in the bottom of the twelfth when Killefer walked home from third while the Cubs were arguing a disputed error at first base.

September 1 A three-way pennant race—Brooklyn, Philadelphia, and Boston—was waxing hot. On this day 19,000 fans packed Baker Bowl for a doubleheader against the league-leading Brooklyns. By then Alexander had pitched 13 shutouts, tying the single-season record held by Jack Coombs, who, fittingly, was his opponent on the mound in the first game.

There were many palpitations as the visiting hostiles began the second inning with two singles. Mowrey attempted to sacrifice, but Killefer made a diving catch of the bunt. Excitement continued as Ivy Olson (.254) doubled to left. Whitted was on it like a cat and threw an airborne strike to the plate, nailing the fleet-footed Wheat by several feet. Otto Miller (.255) then lifted a fly, ending the frame.

In the eighth, Olson reached on Bancroft's error. Miller flied out, but the unlikely Coombs doubled to left, Olson stopping at third. Manager Wilbert Robinson summoned Jim Hickman to run for Coombs. It was for naught, however, as Myers hit a shot back at Pete, who turned quickly to catch Olson off third. Stengel then ended the afternoon's titillation by flying out.

Eppa Rixey pitched a shutout in the second game also, pulling the home team up to just three games behind the league leaders.

THE STRETCH DRIVE

September 16 Alex's near miss (see above) put the Phils in second place, 1.5 games behind the Robins.

September 19 Another near-miss, this one a 2–0 loss, put Philadelphia two games behind Brooklyn.

September 23 Pete raised the pennant hopes of Philadelphians as he won a doubleheader in just two and a half hours to bring himself a $100 bonus and bring his team within 1.5 games of Brooklyn. "A great cry rang out when it was seen that Alex would pitch the second game," which was his fifteenth shutout (see above). The Nebraskan seemed to strengthen as the day wore on. He told trainer Mike Dee that he felt he could have pitched a third game.

September 28 Trailing by 1.5 games, the Phillies invaded Brooklyn for three games. As usual, Alexander pitched the opening contest and coasted to an 8–4 win. The Quakers were now just a half game behind.

September 30 After a rainout, Eppa Rixey won the morning game to put the Phils into first by half a game. The nightcap was a nightmare. Alexander was hammered for 11 hits and lost, 6–1. Even more devastating was the season-ending injury to Bancroft, the glue of the Phils' defense.

October 2 Before a packed house at Baker Bowl against third-place Boston, Alex won his 16th shutout and pitched the Phillies into first place again. But they lost the second game, 4–1, as Milt Stock, Bancroft's replacement, made a costly error.

October 3 The Braves won a doubleheader on costly errors to fall 2.5 games behind with two games remaining. However, headlines roared charges that perhaps the Giants had thrown their two games to the Dodgers. The Phils hoped the two Giant games would be replayed and summoned Alexander to pitch one more time, October 4. He responded with his third save of the season. But the disputed games were never replayed, and the Dodgers were awarded the pennant.

Baseball's worst team?

Why Connie Mack's Hair Turned White

GEORGE KOCHANOWICZ

Mayor Curley of Boston had just thrown out the first ball of the season, as the twenty-one-year-old southpaw strode to the mound at Fenway Park to begin the Red Sox' defense of their 1915 world championship. One hour and fifty-five minutes later Babe Ruth had his first of 23 victories as the Red Sox edged out the Athletics, 2–1. The loss was the first of 117 for the Athletics.

The previous year they had lost 109 games, a result of Connie Mack's breakup of his dynastic 1914 American League champions.

Just two years earlier the pitching staff was anchored by Bob Shawkey, Eddie Plank, Herb Pennock, and Chief Bender. Shawkey and Pennock were traded. Plank and Bender defected to the Federal League. Of the $100,000 in-field, Eddie Collins, Jack Barry, and Frank Baker were all traded. Outfielder Honest Eddie Murphy was traded. Connie Mack chose to trade his 1914 AL champions for lesser players and cash rather than lose them to Federal League raiders. Their suspicious performance in the 1914 World Series, being swept by the Miracle Boston Braves, has also been rumored to be a reason for their departure.

When the 1916 Athletics left their spring training base at Jacksonville, Florida, to barnstorm north, they probably suspected that disaster lay ahead. They had won only 43 games in 1915.

The season opened at Boston with two losses. Following a winless stay in New York, the Athletics opened at home, losing to Boston 7–1. Their first win was against the Red Sox the next afternoon, 3–1. That year they lost twenty straight games. In another depressing stretch they lost nineteen straight on the road.

Just two years later, they would finish with a 36–117 record for a percentage of .235, the lowest in this century.

Was this the worst team in modern history?
Probably.

In an eight-team league they finished 40 games behind the seventh-place Washington Senators, the only other team in the league below .500 at 76–77.

At one point the Athletics lost twenty games in a row. Their shortstop committed 78 errors. Two of their starting pitchers had a combined record of 2 wins and 36 losses. The team made 314 errors, or an average of two per game.

It's not easy to lose 117 games. Connie Mack employed

Amos Strunk

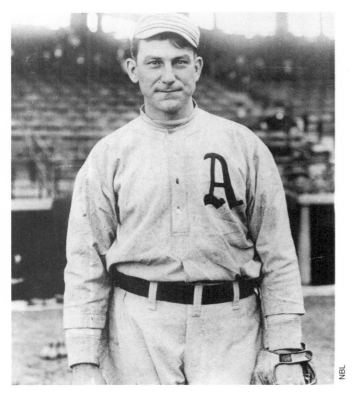

Nap Lajoie

Rookie righthander Elmer Myers had his best seasons of his career, throwing 315 innings with 182 strikeouts and 31 complete games, both figures second in the league to Walter Johnson. His record was 14–23, aided by a league-leading 168 walks.

Jack Nabors, a twenty-eight-year-old righthander who compiled a 3.47 ERA, was rewarded with 1 win and 19 losses. The fourth starter, twenty-two-year-old righthander Tom Sheehan, had a 3.69 ERA and a 1–16 record. The staff led the league in both complete games and walks.

It got to the point, according to Tom Sheehan, that Nabors, after seeing Sheehan lose a one-hitter in the opener of a doubleheader at Boston, chose to throw a deliberate wild pitch in the ninth inning of the second game with the score tied 1–1, and the winning run on third base. Sheehan asked Nabors why he threw that one away. Jack replied, "Look, I knew those guys wouldn't get me another run, and if you think I'm going to throw nine more innings on a hot day like this, you're crazy."

Strangely, the season ended with the Athletics taking both ends of a doubleheader against the champion Red Sox. The Sox were resting their starters for the upcoming World Series against Brooklyn.

Rumor has it that 1916 was the year that Cornelius McGilicuddy's hair started turning white.

fifty players to accomplish the feat. The youngest of the Athletics was seventeen-year-old Charlie Grimm, who hit two singles in 22 at bats. Charlie later managed the Chicago Cubs and Milwaukee Braves. The oldest was forty-year-old Nap Lajoie, who was winding up a twenty-one-year career, hitting .246, his range at second base was greatly reduced.

The Athletics best player was center fielder Amos Strunk who enjoyed one of his best seasons of his career, with .316. Catcher-outfielder Wally Schang had a good year, hitting 7 homers in only 338 at bats, tied for third in the league behind the Yankees' Wally Pipp, who hit 12, and the Yankees' Frank (Home Run) Baker—a former A—who hit 10.

The Athletics weakest area, among their many, seemed to be their infield defense. At shortstop was twenty-year-old Whitey Witt who made 78 errors. Whitey later found his niche with the Yankees, playing center field alongside Babe Ruth. Whitey's keystone partner was Nap Lajoie, whose immobility permitted only 16 errors at second base. At the hot corner, Charlie Pick made 42 errors.

The Athletics strong point, if any, was probably their pitching, despite their ERA of 3.84, highest in the league. The horrendous infield defense, especially the lack of range of Lajoie, was partially responsible.

The ace of the staff was twenty-three-year-old Bullet Joe Bush, who six years later compiled a 26–7 record for the 1922 Yankees. In 1914 Bush had a 16–2 record. In 1916 he fell to 15–22 despite an ERA of 2.57.

Bullet Joe Bush

The first of many at Ebbets Field

A World Series for Flatbush

RICHARD GOLDSTEIN

Casey Stengel squeezed his glove on the flyball off the bat of Duffy Lewis, and then madness reigned. Thousands of fans swarmed onto the Ebbets Field grass, yelling, snake-dancing, and tossing straw cushions. A pair of revelers unfurled a green banner with the emblem of a baseball, the official flag of their beloved Brooklyn team.

Dodger *green*?

It was Tuesday, October 10, 1916. The Brooklyn Dodgers had just beaten the Boston Red Sox, 4–3, for their first victory ever in a "modern" World Series game.

The Brooklyn franchise, dating back to 1883, when it debuted as a minor league team, had been in formal postseason play only twice before. Back in 1889, as a member of the American Association, Brooklyn had lost in the old-time World Series to the National League's Giants as baseball's greatest rivalry was born. In 1890, a Brooklyn team newly arrived in the National League played Louisville of the American Association to a World Series deadlock (three victories apiece and a tie) before cold weather and dwindling fan interest prematurely sent everybody home for the winter.

The Dodgers had fallen on hard times in the early years of the twentieth century, but their luck changed in 1916. Wilbert Robinson, the portly, profane, and often bumbling manager known fondly as Uncle Robbie, had assembled a cast good enough to take the pennant by two-and-a-half games over the Phillies.

Jake Daubert, one of the league's top hitters, was the first baseman. George Cutshaw, a fine fielder, held down second base. Ivy Olson, a spirited lad who had once been ejected from an intrasquad spring training game for throwing sand on an umpire, played shortstop. The soon-to-be-forgotten Mike Mowrey was at third. Zack Wheat, en route to the Hall of Fame, was a fixture in left field, Hi Myers played center, and Casey Stengel, in his fourth full season and already a "character," was around in right. Otto Miller shared the catching with Chief Meyers, a former Giant who helped develop a fine pitching staff at the Polo Grounds when Uncle Robbie had coached there under John McGraw.

Rube Marquard, Larry Cheney, Jack Coombs, Wheezer Dell, and Sherry Smith. Nap Rucker, an outstanding lefty, had finally ruined his arm after a decade pitching for a succession of miserable Brooklyn ball clubs, and was in his last season at age thirty-one.

On their way to the pennant, the Dodgers found themselves enmeshed in fisticuffs away from Ebbets Field and controversy at the ballpark.

Nathan Handwerker opened Nathan's Famous at Coney Island in 1916, enjoying instant success for his venture by dropping the price of a hot dog from the customary ten cents to a nickel. But for Casey Stengel, Coney brought misadventure that summer. After a bunch of Brooklyn players had enjoyed a fine time at the beach amid more than a few beers, Casey got into a brawl with Whitey Appleton, a Dodger pitcher. Stengel and Appleton, swathed in bandages the next day, concocted a tale of accidentally falling down a flight of stairs together.

Jack Coombs, left, and Uncle Robbie

On the afternoon of October 3, it was John McGraw who was ready to level some punches—not at the Dodgers but his own ballplayers. The Dodgers played the Giants at Ebbets Field that Tuesday with three games to go in the season and a chance to clinch the pennant over Philadelphia.

The Giants scored three runs in the first inning off lefty Sherry Smith, but soon the Dodgers routed Giant starter Rube Benton. Then his teammates went into a swoon. Relief pitcher Pol Perritt, ignoring McGraw's orders, used a full windup with men on base. Easy grounders went through the Giant infielders and the team ran the bases brainlessly. An enraged McGraw left the ballpark in the fifth inning with the Dodgers leading, 6–5. They went on to win by 9–6, giving Jeff Pfeffer his 25th victory and the noisy Brooklyn fans a long-sought pennant.

McGraw, while stopping short of accusing his ballplayers of a "fix," pronounced himself "disgusted." He headed south, spending the last two days of the season betting on the ponies at Laurel racetrack in Maryland. The Phillies' manager, Pat Moran, demanded an investigation of the Giants' performance, but the National League president, John K. Tener, maintained that every Giant player "was fighting tooth and nail." There would be no inquiry.

Dodger-Giant enmity notwithstanding, McGraw's men may have had motivation to dump the game. A number of Giant players had kind feelings toward Uncle Robbie from his days as a Giant coach. And there had been ill will between the Giants and the Phillies stemming from recent on-field brawls.

The Dodgers may have entered the World Series under a cloud, but all was sunshine for their fans. Brooklynites lined their streets to cheer the players on as they rode in an eighteen-car caravan from Ebbets Field to Grand Central Terminal. Some 5,000 fans provided a sendoff at the terminal for the rail trip to Boston.

The Red Sox won the opener, 6–5, at Braves Field, borrowed from the National Leaguers because it had a bigger capacity than Fenway Park. Boston also took Game Two in one of the great pitching duels in Series history as a young lefty named Babe Ruth bested Sherry Smith in a 2–1 game that went fourteen innings.

So the Dodgers returned to Ebbets Field down 2 games to 0. Back in October 1916, the ballpark—opened four years earlier in a then-desolate northern fringe of the Flatbush neighborhood—only vaguely resembled the shape it would ultimately take. The double-deck stands extended from the right field foul pole to midway between third base and the left field pole. An open concrete grandstand was located along the left field line and wooden bleachers were placed beyond the left field and center field fences. The landmark right field scoreboard would not be erected until the early 1930s. Abe Stark was only twenty years old in the autumn of 1916, and if he envisioned a "Hit Sign, Win Suit" advertisement guarding Bedford Avenue, he was keeping his thoughts to himself.

The afternoon of Game Three came up chilly with a brisk wind. Some 21,087 fans—about 3,000 short of capacity—turned out, bundled in overcoats, sweaters, and even furs. They rang cowbells, whistled and cheered mightily when Ivy Olson slammed a two-run triple in the fifth inning off submariner Carl Mays. Jake Daubert added three hits and Jack Coombs, with relief help from Jeff Pfeffer, got the victory.

But for Brooklyn, it was all downhill from there. Boston's Dutch Leonard outpitched Rube Marquard in Game Four, the Red Sox winning by 6–2. Then the clubs went back to Boston, where the Red Sox wrapped up the championship on Columbus Day with a 4–1 victory before 42,620, the largest crowd that had ever turned out for a World Series game.

The Dodgers would plunge to seventh place the following season. They wouldn't win another pennant until 1920, and then they would fall in the World Series to the Cleveland Indians, victimized in the bargain by Bill Wambsganss's unassisted triple play.

Brooklyn's Rube Marquard, who lost Games One and Four in the World Series of 1916, would have an even more embarrassing time in the 1920 Series. Not only would he lose the opener, but he was arrested at a Cleveland hotel for trying to scalp tickets. Ivy Olson, Brooklyn's hero in Game Four of the '16 Series, would also go on to ignoble moments. His fumbling in the field would eventually bring so much razzing from the Brooklyn fans that he would show up at Ebbets Field with cotton stuffed in his ears.

Zack Wheat takes a cut for the camera.

Baseball's most famous suspect

The Prince of Darkness

MARTIN DONELL KOHOUT

On Sunday, April 16, 1916, some 18,000 Cincinnatians came out to Redland Field to watch the Reds play the Pittsburgh Pirates. They howled when the home team's first baseman, Fred Mollwitz, was ejected in the third inning for arguing a called strike. Reds manager Buck Herzog sent up the veteran Prince Hal Chase, who had joined the team only a day earlier, to complete Mollwitz's at bat, with the count no balls and two strikes and a runner on second base.

Chase lashed the first pitch into left field for a double, driving in Cincinnati's third run of the game, then stole third base. After the next batter walked, Chase stole home on the front end of a double steal. The Reds went on to win 6–1 and the city of Cincinnati had a new sporting hero.

Chase had followed a long and tortuous road to Cincinnati. Although he was a solid hitter (a .291 career batting average) and outstanding baserunner (363 stolen bases), he was one of those rare stars known primarily for his spectacular defense, like Ozzie Smith or Keith Hernandez in more recent years. His peers considered Chase the greatest first baseman in baseball history, but in his ten previous major league seasons, mostly spent with New York, he had also earned a reputation as an inveterate troublemaker.

This reputation was richly deserved. In 1908 he had jumped the Highlanders to play outlaw ball in his native California, and two New York managers, George Stallings in 1910 and Frank Chance in 1913, had accused him of "laying down" on the team. Chase convinced Highlander owner Frank Farrell to fire Stallings and appoint him as Stallings's successor, an experiment that lasted only one full season and resulted in a sixth-place finish, but Chance succeeded in trading him to Chicago.

Chase jumped the White Sox for Buffalo of the upstart Federal League in 1914 and became one of the Feds' biggest stars. He batted .347 in the second half of the 1914 season and led the league with 17 home runs in 1915. But after the Federal League ceased operations, Chase spent the spring of 1916 practicing with the San Francisco Seals of the Pacific Coast League.

Ban Johnson, still seething at Chase's jump to the Feds, had vowed that he would never play in the American League again. Because of Chase's reputation, no National League team seemed willing to take him on either. Although he was

Hal Chase

BRACE

only thirty-three and coming off two outstanding seasons, his major league career appeared to be over.

An angel finally appeared in the jovial person of August (Garry) Herrmann, chairman of the National Commission and president of the Reds. The Reds had never won a pennant and in the previous three seasons had finished seventh, eighth, and seventh; an attraction such as Prince Hal would be most welcome in Cincinnati. The Reds spent the winter insisting that they would not sign Chase unless Mollwitz's arm problems recurred. In early April, Jack Ryder of the Cincinnati *Enquirer* had reported confidently that "Moll's wing has been doing efficient service so far and it looks as if he will be able to get through the season all right," Three days later the Reds announced that they had offered Chase a contract.

"There is no great enthusiasm around town over the signing of the former American League star," reported Ryder. "That Chase is the most sensational of all first basemen is the undisputed truth," but Prince Hal's reputation as a troublemaker and contract jumper made Cincinnati fans wary.

Chase's reaction to Cincinnati's offer was also underwhelming: "I have not made up my mind just what I am going to do. It is possible that I would prefer to remain in California, even if there is no chance to play ball. At all events, I am in no hurry to decide,"

Having thought things over, he finally arrived in Cincinnati on April 15, looking "exuberantly healthy." The Reds had won three of their first four games without him, however, and Herzog was unwilling to break up a winning lineup by putting Mollwitz on the bench—until the umpire forced his hand.

From May 18 to June 13, Chase hit safely in nineteen straight games, and his glovework was as dazzling as ever, even when he spent a month playing the outfield after injuries left the Reds shorthanded. In late April, Ryder proclaimed him "the fastest and smartest first baseman in the business," and in early June he wrote that "Hal has a knack of doing the right thing at the right time that marks him as a winning player."

The Reds were still in fourth place in late May, with a 19–21 record, but by mid-July they had lost 28 of their last 41 games and had tumbled into the National League cellar. In the middle of this horrible slump Herzog was said to be "in the depths of despair." The Reds' efforts to trade him became common knowledge.

On the morning of July 20, the *Enquirer* ran a photograph of Chase and identified him as the "Reds' New Manager," but later that day Herrmann traded Herzog and outfielder Wade Killefer to the Giants for infielder Bill McKechnie, outfielder Edd Roush, and Christy Mathewson, who took over as manager of the team.

The Reds lost 14 of their first 18 games under Mathewson, but Herrmann had promised to be patient, and most Cincinnati fans realized that Matty was taking over a demoralized ballclub. All through this dreadful streak, however, Chase continued to hit. By August 13, after the Reds had split six games in Philadelphia, he had 10 hits in his last 23 at bats to raise his batting average to .318.

At the beginning of September, Chase was seventh in the league in batting, with a .307 average. Brooklyn's Jake Daubert was first, at .325, with Rogers Hornsby of St. Louis second at .319. By September 11, with the Reds in New York to begin their final Eastern trip, Chase was atop the National League batting race with a .320 average. He sounded quietly confident about holding that position: "I have always hit well on all the Eastern grounds, with the exception of Boston. We are going to run up against tough pitching on this trip, but I think I can hold my own."

In fact he did more than that, batting .418 over his last 18 games (including a 7-for-14 performance in three games in Boston) and raising his final average to .339. The Reds finished the season in Cincinnati on Sunday, October 1, with a 4–0 victory over the Pirates to tie the Cardinals for seventh place. Before the game, in which Chase doubled and singled, he was honored in a ceremony at home plate featuring comely actress May Buckley.

Chase finished second (by one) in runs batted in (82) and slugging percentage (.459). He led the Reds in runs (66), doubles (29), home runs (4), and stolen bases (22).

The 1916 season provided a glimpse of the player that Hal Chase should have been, but he never approached such heights again. The Reds rose to fourth place in 1917, then to third in 1918. Before the end of the latter season, however, Mathewson suspended him for offering bribes to teammates to throw games. Inexplicably exonerated by National League president John Heydler, an unrepentant Chase was traded to the Giants before the 1919 season. Back in New York he proceeded to betray the trust of his old friend John McGraw and to play a role, as yet undetermined, in setting up the infamous Black Sox fix.

Chase was forced out of the major leagues after the 1919 season and returned to California to play in the independent Mission League. After being banned in California for his alleged involvement in yet another bribery scandal, this one involving Pacific Coast League players, he drifted down to Arizona, where he played semipro ball in a number of dusty mining towns along the Mexican border. He began to drink heavily, and when age and alcohol caught up with him, he became a virtual derelict, working odd jobs and sponging off acquaintances. He died on May 18, 1947, in Colusa, California, stubbornly insisting to the last that he was innocent of the various charges against him.

Speaker in Cleveland

A Letter From the Attic

Not long ago, a Boston woman (she requests anonymity) discovered in her attic a bundle of yellowed letters to her deceased grandfather from his boyhood friend who had emigrated to Cleveland at the turn of the century. Because the letters dealt exhaustively with baseball, she donated the cache to SABR.

Robert Carr
Cleveland, Ohio
Friday, October 13, 1916

Dear Beaneater:

Congratulations! This morning's *Plain Dealer* reports the obvious: your Red Sox are world champions again. But sending us Tris Speaker last spring almost cost you the pennant. World Series euphoria may obscure Boston's 10-game sag…

1915	101–53
1916	91–63

Speaker led the Indians to a 18-game improvement…

1915	57–95
1916	77–77

True, we finished sixth, but as late as July 12 we were in first place. I saved boxscores, made my own calculations—couldn't wait for *The Sporting News*—and can tell you Tris hit .390 against you. Versus New York, he batted .463.

Enthusiasm soared here last April when we learned Spoke was headed west. Joe Lannin [Sox owner] may have made wagonloads of money in the hotel business, but he muffed this deal. He tried to cut Speaker's salary after Boston won the Series in 1915 and after Speaker, the best center fielder anywhere, had been again the only .300 batsman in your lineup. From $15,000 to $9,000, rumor has it. No wonder Tris was a holdout all spring.

Tris Speaker comes in for one.

Speaker is a reasonable man. He knew he had the highest salary in the league. He said he'd consider a cut. But not that much. Maybe he'd take $12,000. Tris showed his sincerity by training with the Sox, though he wouldn't sign.

Remember how *The Sporting News* roasted Speaker? Comments like… now that the bidding war with the Federal League is over, Speaker ought to be grateful he plays for such a generous, farsighted owner.

Then—bingo!—just before Opening Day, Lannin's patience ran out. For his best and most popular player, he got $50,000, plus Sad Sam Jones and Tommy Thomas. Jones hasn't won a game yet for Boston, and Thomas is an infielder somewhere in the minors.

Everyone here expected Jim Dunn (he'd owned the Indians for about two weeks) to dismiss Lee Fohl and make Speaker the Indian chief. Well, not yet.

In the outfield, Tris is boss. Before almost every pitch, he tosses grass in the air, gauges the breezes, and gestures Jack Graney and Bobby Roth hither and yon.

Did you know this trio led the league in assists? 67! Speaker 25. Graney 22. Roth 20. No longer can Boston claim the best throwing outfield. Lewis, Walker, and Hooper rang up only 47.

Speaker still frightens us by playing shallow for everyone. I heard him tell a businessmen's group the odds favor this tactic. The number of Texas Leaguers he prevents will outweigh the drives he can't outrun in deep center.

Sometimes, when a sacrifice bunt is imminent, Tris sprints in to cover second. He explains this move allows both the first baseman and the third baseman to rush the plate, while the second baseman covers first and the shortstop covers third.

Wish you could see him dash back into League Park's spacious c.f. and left-center. Ray Chapman was quoted, soon after the trade: "Boys, we have three good outfielders, but Tris Speaker can cover almost twice as much ground as any of them." He plays the r.f. wall smartly, too—just as he did your wall in Fenway. (No ads on ours!)

Tris captured fans' hearts all over town. We see him at the Hollenden, where he stays, and in his automobile—a small T.E.S. on its sides—and at shows at Playhouse Square. Jim Dunn wanted Speaker to go to work for the Dunn-McCarthy Construction Company, but so far our hero has limited his salesmanship to the Cleveland Baseball Club. Tris attends a great many gatherings and makes a winning appearance. I like his voice—a deep rumble with a Texas twang—and I like his customary opening statement, too: "I'm a Speaker, but I'm no talker."

Isn't it a relief to have someone other than Cobb lead the league? Nine years in a row! Let's hope we see more lists like this…

Tris Speaker, Cleve.	.386
Ty Cobb, Det.	.371
Joe Jackson, Chi.	.341

Sam Jones, demonstrating how he got his nickname

Amos Strunk, Phila.	.316
Eddie Collins, Chi.	.308
Larry Gardner, Bos.	.308

I saved a *Plain Dealer* editorial from April 11: "The Coming of Speaker"… "everyone has assumed a larger optimism. Sixth City will not be good enough to satisfy anyone now. The coming to Cleveland of one of the very few first-class players in America has caused the change… one of the half dozen brightest stars of the baseball skies. Not since Napoleon Lajoie, away back in ancient times, made baseball history by jumping to Cleveland have the Cleveland devotees had *so delicious a shock*… East 66th Street may again become a center of civic pride and joy."

Prophetic words! Attendance more than tripled—to almost half a million.

Must close. I'm mailing $2.75 to Mr. Spink. *The Sporting News* is offering 75 photographs with a year's renewal.

Your old pal,
Bob

Okay, okay, Cleveland's Bob Carr is still with us, and still—with friends Fred Schuld and Dick Derby—mining Indian facts and stats from the past.

Red Sox repeat as champs

The Babe Saves Boston's Season

RICHARD "DIXIE" TOURANGEAU

Red Sox manager Bill "Rough" Carrigan handed the baseball to twenty-one-year old Babe Ruth on Opening Day, 1916. A variety of circumstances had put the pressure of hurling the season opener squarely on the Babe's shoulders.

The defending champion Red Sox had already lost Smoky Joe Wood (15–5 with a league-leading 1.48 ERA) to a permanent sore arm. Their ace, Ernie Shore (19–8, 1.64), also complained of a painful arm. And their biggest gun, Tris Speaker (.322), had just been traded to Cleveland.

No one would have guessed how well Babe would carry the load right up to the year's finale.

The kid had sported an 18–8 record in '15, and his four home runs in then huge Fenway Park had led the team. Yet Babe hadn't even been used in the World Series against the Phils in October.

The 1916 opener, against the Philadelphia A's Jack Nabors, was the beginning of a remarkable season for Babe. He went on to a 23–12 season and led the Sox to the pennant over Chicago and Detroit.

As September began, Ruth was 17–11, and Boston was in first, three and a half games ahead of Chicago. But they would be on the road for almost the entire month. Ruth saved his best for the stretch. He won six in a row, never giving more than two runs a game, and hurled the Red Sox to the pennant.

After he beat New York, 7–1, both Boston teams were in first, and wild Hub fans dreamed of a city Series. But within a few days the Braves slumped to third. Meanwhile, Carrigan's troops had but a two-game edge over the surging Detroit Tigers.

Boston faced consecutive three-game sets at Chicago and Detroit. When the Red Sox arrived in Chicago, the three teams were virtually tied. The Red Sox lost the opener, falling to third place, a half-game out.

The next day Comiskey Park was packed to see Ruth duel Red Faber (17–9). Spectators on the outfield grass nearly spelled doom for Ruth as Eddie Collins (.308) and Joe Jackson (.341) got hits into the fans and scored in the first. But Ruth gave up only two more hits, and Harry Hooper's bases-loaded single in the second ignited Boston's 6–2 win.

The Red Sox won the final game in Chicago and swept all three in Detroit.

As the days dwindled down, Ruth shut out Speaker (.385) and sixth-place Cleveland to put the Red Sox in first to stay. Upon returning to Fenway he just about clinched the pennant with a 3–0 victory over the fourth-place Yankees and their ace, Bob Shawkey (24–14). It was Ruth's ninth shutout.

Babe's won-lost record at this point was 23–11 with a 1.66 ERA. He ended the season with a tuneup for the World Series against the A's, the most dreadful team of this century. He gave up four runs in five innings to end at 23–12 and 1.75.

He gave up no home runs in 324 innings.

Ruth was 6–3 against the two other contenders. He won two out of three against Chicago, which finished two games in the rear. He won four out of six against the Tigers, who finished third, four games behind. Babe held Ty Cobb to a .250 average. In fact, the Tigers, the best-hitting team in the league at .264, hit only .170 against the Babe.

Ruth also beat Walter Johnson (25–20 with seventh-place Washington) four times, including two 1–0 games.

THE WORLD SERIES

Boston won the opening game against the Dodgers, 6–5.

Ruth toed the mound for Game Two in new Braves Field before a record Series crowd of 41,373. Twenty thousand others jammed Boston's bustling "Newspaper Row" for inning-by-inning accounts. In Worcester thousands watched the game re-created on a huge board called "The Thriller."

The game began under hovering dark clouds in a mild 75-degree temperature. Behind the plate was umpire Bill Dinneen, who had hurled three shutouts for the Red Sox in the first NL - AL World Series in 1903.

Brooklyn manager Wilbert Robinson benched lefthanded Casey Stengel, who had had two hits in Game One and would lead all batters in the Series with .364.

Ruth got Stengel's replacement, righthanded Jimmy Johnston (.252) and Brooklyn's top hitter, lefty Jake Daubert

(.316), on easy fly balls. Then centerfielder Hy Myers stepped into the box, hitting .262 with three home runs, all of them inside the park.

On a ball-one count, Myers lined a pitch between right fielder Harry Hooper and Tilly Walker, who had replaced Speaker as Boston's center fielder. Hooper made a spectacular headlong dive but missed. The ball skipped all the way to the special "50-cent standee" fence and bounced back toward Walker, who slipped on some wet grass. Myers "ran like a scared deer" around the bases and dove head-first across home plate, as visiting Brooklyn rooters went crazy banging pans and bells.

It was the only homer Babe gave up all year.

Brooklyn lost a chance for another run in the third. The opposing hurler, Sherry Smith, hooked a Babe pitch down the right-field line, where hustling Hooper made a perfect throw to relay man Walker, who in turn threw to third. Smith, running with his head down, was out by plenty. If he'd stayed on second, he might have scored, as Johnston followed with a clean single. Brooklyn scribes blamed third base coach Colby Jack Coombs, a New Englander and former American Leaguer, for the mental error.

Still wheezing from his run, Smith faced Boston's first batter, Everett Scott (.232), who, falling away from a pitch, stung a triple between the outfielders—Scotty had managed only two triples all year. After a ground out, Ruth himself chopped a grounder to second baseman George Cutshaw, who fumbled it as the tying run scored.

Ruth could have put his team ahead in the fifth. Boston's Pinch Thomas whacked a drive over Zack Wheat's head, and when shortstop Ivy Olson tripped Thomas, umpire Ernie Quigly awarded him a triple. Opportunity knocked loudly, but Ruth whiffed.

In the Brooklyn eighth, Coombs played it cautious. Mike Mowrey (.244) singled and was sacrificed. Catcher Otto Miller (.255) singled sharply, and Walker's throw home was wide. But Coombs had held Mowrey at third.

Boston got another break in the last of the ninth when Wheat, after a long run, couldn't hold onto a curving fly by Harold Janvrin (.293), who got a double.

Then Carrigan made a bold move. He lifted the righthanded batting Walker (.266) and put in lefty Jimmy Walsh (.229) against the lefthanded Smith. Walsh slapped one back to Smith, who threw to third sacker Mowrey. Janvrin's hard slide jarred the ball from Mike's grasp.

Brooklyn seemed doomed. But a bit of luck—and Hy Myers—saved them again. Instead of bunting, Dick Hoblitzell (.259) decided to swing, sending a fly ball to center field. Myers acted as if he had lost it in the sun but grabbed the ball and uncorked a marvelous white streak to catch the sliding Janvrin.

In the bottom of the tenth, the sun peeked through the clouds one last time, as Scott led off with a single. Thomas sacrificed and Ruth, trying to knock the ball into the Charles River, whiffed again. A collective "Oh" was audible from the crowd. Hooper singled down the third base line, but fast-thinking Mowrey bluffed a throw to first and tossed to shortstop Ivy Olson, who was alertly tending third, to put Scott out when he overslid the bag.

Ruth seemed weary, but he got through the eleventh and twelfth as the afternoon grew darker.

The game surpassed the two previous longest Series games, both twelve frames.

In the thirteenth, Mowrey reached on an error, was sacrificed, and with two outs, Smith had another chance to win his own game. His sinking smash to left-center was caught by a sprinting Duffy Lewis, another Red Sox defensive gem that broke Brooklyn hearts.

The darkness made following the ball very difficult, and the crowd sensed that the fourteenth would be the last inning. Hoblitzell walked and was sacrificed, and Carrigan fearlessly played all his trump cards.

He pinch-hit righty-swinging Del "Ducky" Gainor (.254) for his best batter, Larry Gardner (.308), who was 0-for-5 against Smith. Carrigan also called on the speedy Mike McNally of Minooka, Pennsylvania to pinch-run. By then the ball was "as black as ink," but after a swinging strike, Gainor, in his only at bat in the Series, lined a single to left, and Wheat's off-balance throw home was too late.

Babe finally got his shower, having thrown 148 pitches. (Smith had thrown exactly the same.)

Gainor's single cost each team $75,000, the amount that a replay of a tie game would have meant in their coffers.

Boston went on to win two of the next three games and the championship.

In 1918 Babe would add 16⅔ more scoreless Series innings for a record of 29⅔, a mark that remained unbroken until Whitey Ford passed it in 1962.

THE BABE AT BAT in 1916

Babe hit only three home runs that season, all of them on the road and all within six at bats. Fenway's center field was 488 feet away then. Only two homers were hit in Fenway all year, by Boston's Tillie Walker and Detroit's Bobby Veach—and one of those was inside the park.

Ruth's first homer, June 9 off Detroit righthander Jean Dubuc (10–10) was called "one of the longest drives ever seen in Navin Field." Babe pinch-hit his second one three days later against Jim Park (1–4) at St. Louis, and his third next day against the Browns' Dave Davenport (12–11).

On September 12 in Washington, outfielder Clyde "Deerfoot" Milan went into deep center field to rob Ruth of a fourth homer.

Babe Ruth in 1916
44 games, 324 innings , 23–12

Date	Opp	Rank	W-L	Score	Comment
Apr 12	Phi	8	W	2–1	4 hitter vs Nabors (1–20 in '16)
Apr 17	Was	7	W	5–1	beat Johnson (25–10, 1.89)
Apr 20	Phi	8 A	W	7–1	
Apr 25	NY	4 A	W	4–3	10 inn
May 1	Was	7 A	L	3–5	9 walks
May 5	NY	4	-	4–8	blew 4–0 lead; team lost in 13th
May 10	Cle	6	L	2–6	Speaker (.386) 2 hits, 3 runs
May 20	StL	5	W	3–1	2 hits, left with bases loaded 6th
May 24	Det	3	W	4–0	Hooper 4 great catches; Babe loaded bases in 2nd, pitched out of jam
May 27	NY	4 A	L	2–4	
Jun 1	Was	7	W	1–0	3-hitter vs Johnson; Babe fanned twice
Jun 5	Cle	6 A	W	5–0	
Jun 9	Det	3 A	-	5–6	Ruth HR; blew 4–1 lead in 8th
Jun 13	StL	5 A	W	5–3	Ruth HR
Jun 17	Chi	2 A	L	0–5	Joe Jackson (.341) 3 hits
Jun 22	NY	4	W	1–0	3-hitter, 2 by Gilhooley (..278)
Jun 27	Phi	8	W	7–2	10 strikeouts
Jul 1	Was	7 A	L	2–4	KO'd in 4th
Jul 7	Cle	6	-	2–1	left in 7th with 1–1 tie
Jul 11	Chi	0	-		pitched to first batter only
Jul 11	Chi	2	W	3–1	
Jul 15	StL	5	W	17–4	
Jul 18	StL	5	W	4–3	Ruth triple, 2 runs
Jul 20	Det	3	L	2–3	5 IP relief; lost in 13th to H. Coveleskie (20–11) on Cobb (.371) leg hit, Ruth's own error

Date	Opp	Rank	W-L	Score	Comment
Jul 25	Cle	6 A	L	4–5	Speaker 3 hits, 2 runs
Jul 29	Det	3 A	L	8–10	KO'd in 1st
Jul 31	Det	3 A	W	6–0	beat Coveleskie on 2 hits (Cobb and Burns (.286)
Aug 4	StL	5 A	L	1–6	Plank (16–15) threw 2-hitter
Aug 12	Was	7	-	2–1	left in 7th losing 1–0; Johnson lost in relief
Aug 15	Was	7	W	1–0	beat Johnson in 13th; Milan robbed him of HR
Aug 19	Cle	6	-	2–1	left with score 1–1 relief
Aug 23	Cle	2	-	7–3	relief
Aug 24	Det	3	W	3–0	beat Coveleskie on 3-hitter
Aug 29	StL	5	L	3–5	5 IP in relief; left with bases filled; Babe fanned with sacks full
Aug 31	StL	5	L	1–2	
Sep 4	NY	4 A	W	7–1	started fabulous September run
Sep 5	Phi	4 A	–	5–2	relief
Sep 9	Was	7 A	W	2–1	4-hitter beat Johnson fourth time
Sep 12	Was	7 A	-	3–4	blew 1–0 lead in 9th; Milan grabbed another HR bid; Johnson finally be at Sox
Sep 17	Chi	2 A	W	6–2	beat Faber (17–9)
Sep 21	Det	3 A	W	10–2	Ruth tripled
Sep 25	Cle	6 A	W	2–0	
Sep 29	NY	4	W	3–0	beat Shawkey (24–14)
Oct 2	Phi	8	L	5–7	pennant clinched, hurled 5 innings as Series warmup: 4 runs, 11 hits

TEAM-BY-TEAM RECAP:

Opp	Rank	W–L	BA
Chi	2	2–1	.212
Det	3	4–2	.170
NY	4	4–1	.196
StL	5	4–3	.196
Cle	6	2–2	.205
Wash	7	4–2	.180
Phil	8	3–1	.256*
Totals		23–12	.199

.213 before the season finale

A record streak, but no championship

26 Straight for McGraw

TOM KNIGHT

The Giants had finished dead last in 1915, but when spring rolled around in 1916, manager John McGraw actually had high hopes of winning the pennant. He figured the Phillies had just had a lucky year in '15 and would not repeat as champions. The New Yorkers went on to have one of the weirdest seasons ever. They were pushovers at times, and unbeatable at other times. They got off to a terrible start, then set a record for consecutive wins on the road. After that they went into a tailspin that would force McGraw to rebuild his club in midseason, then set a record for consecutive victories that has stood for seventy-five years. To top it off, at season's end, the Giants finished fourth beneath a cloud caused by McGraw himself.

McGraw had practically the same team that had finished in the cellar in '15. But he picked up four key men from the folded Federal League. He bought colorful outfielder Benny Kauff, the league-leading batter with .342, for $30,000, a princely sum in those days. He also obtained pitcher Fred Anderson (19–13), catcher Bill Rariden (.270), and, for another ten grand, outfielder Eddie Roush (.298).

The Giants third baseman, Hans Lobert (.251), was injured in an exhibition game against Yale, and McGraw purchased another Federal Leaguer, Bill McKechnie (.251), to replace him.

On opening day his team consisted of:

1b	Fred Merkle	.299 in 1915
2b	Laughing Larry Doyle	.320 to lead NL
ss	Art Fletcher	.254
3b	Bill McKechnie	.251 in FL
of	George Burns	.272
	Benny Kauff	.342 to lead FL
	Dave Robertson	.294
	Edd Roush	.298 in FL
c	Bill Rariden	.270 in FL
p	Fred Anderson	19–13 in FL
	Jeff Tesreau	19–16
	Pol Perritt	12–18
	Ralph Stroud	11–9
	Christy Mathewson	8–14 at age 35
	Rube Schauer	2–8
	Ferdie Schupp	1–0

The team got off to a horrible start. After three weeks, their record was a dismal 1–13. After they won their next game, a Broadway newsboy was silently selling his papers. "Why don't you shout out, 'Giants win!'?" a baseball writer was supposed to have asked.

The boy shrugged: "Who will believe me?"

On May 8 an angry McGraw led his Giants on their first western trip. They surprised everyone by sweeping the Pirates in four games. In Chicago they won three more, then beat the Cardinals three in a row. With a ten-game winning streak, they knocked off the Reds three games and were the talk of baseball. They headed back east to Boston and took the Braves four straight! They now had a 17-game win streak on the road, a major league record.

Memorial Day the Giants went to Philadelphia for a morning and afternoon doubleheader. In the first game, the Giants were behind one run in the eighth inning when Merkle hit a long drive to deep left with two men on. It looked like a home run, but Phillies left fielder Claude Cooper reached over the low wall of the bleachers and made a one-handed catch, and the streak was over. The fact that they knocked Grover Cleveland Alexander (33–12) out of the box and won the second game did not console them.

Now a strange thing happened. The Giants could not win at home. McGraw realized that the streak was a flash in the pan and that his team was going no place. He had to make some changes.

The first deal he made was a shocker. He wanted Reds playing manager Buck Herzog (.267), a former Giant, to play third and traded Mathewson (3–4), McKechnie (.246), and Roush (.188) for him. "It wasn't easy for me to part with Matty," McGraw said. "He not only was the greatest pitcher I ever saw, but he is my friend. However, I'm convinced that his pitching days are over, and he agrees with me. He could stay with the Giants as long as he wanted to, of course. But he is ambitious to become a manager, and I have helped him gratify that ambition."

Herzog fired up the Giants. But McGraw was not finished. He made a deal by telephone that sent another old Polo Grounds favorite, Doyle (hitting .264) to the Cubs for Heinie Zimmerman (.291). Heinie was another live wire, and he

came from the Bronx, just across the river from the Polo Grounds. Zimmerman moved to third base as Herzog took over at second. Doyle had been slowing down, but with Herzog at second, the Giants once again had a good double-play combination.

When the team returned east, another long-time Giant was traded. The slumping Merkle (.237) was sent to Brooklyn, and Walter Holke was recalled from Rochester to play first. Finally, Slim Sallee, a veteran lefthander (5–5) was purchased from the last-place Cardinals.

When September arrived, the Giants were in fourth place, ten games behind the third-place Phillies, as Brooklyn and Boston fought for the lead. On September 7 against Brooklyn at the Polo grounds, the Giants launched the longest winning streak any major league team has ever known.

Giant pitching was overwhelming during the string. They hurled nine shutouts. Righthander Tesreau (18–14 for the year) won six victories, as did lefthanders Schupp (9–3) and Benton (16–8). Schupp posted a one-hitter, two two-hitters, two three-hitters, and a six-hitter. Benton had a one-hitter and a three-hitter. Another righthander, Perritt (18–11), won

Buck Herzog

four in the streak, including two in one day against the Phillies—he gave up only eight hits all day. Pol also hurled in a 1–1 tie.

Sallee, the curveballing lefthander, had been under the weather for a couple of weeks, but when he returned to the lineup September 22, he posted the 17th straight by blanking the Cubs, 5–0. This tied the Giants' own streak racked up in May. The following day the Giants won a doubleheader from the Cardinals to tie the 19-game streak of the White Sox in 1906.

The last-place Cards almost snapped the streak at 22 on September 27. They went into the bottom of the ninth with a 2–0 lead, but the Giants tied it up. Zimmerman opened the tenth with a single. Fletcher (.286) and Kauff (.264) beat out bunts to load the bases, and Zim scored on a wild pitch to win the game.

The Braves came in next and dropped a doubleheader. Kauff helped win the second game with a grand slam. But Boston's Lefty George Tyler (17–10) beat Sallee (9–4 since joining the Giants) to snap the streak at 26 games.

Only one Giant regular finished over .300—Robertson at .307—although Holke hit .351 after being called up. Robertson's 12 homers tied him for the league lead with Cy Williams of the Cubs. Zimmerman led the league with 83 RBI's, while George Burns (.279) led the parade with 105 runs scored.

In spite of the streak, the remarkable Giants still finished fourth, seven games behind the champion Dodgers.

The irascible McGraw was bitter over not winning the pennant. On October 2, the final day of the season, at Ebbets Field, he amazed everyone by leaving the bench before the game ended, claiming his team had not tried to beat the Dodgers. The Giant players were furious and denied the charge to a man; they said they had merely "cooled off" after the amazing winning streak. The press played it up big for a while, and Philadelphia manager Pat Moran demanded an investigation, but the entire episode blew over and was soon forgotten.

McGraw left town for Cuba. There at the race track and other haunts, he sulked away the winter. He came back in 1917 to win the pennant by ten games over the Phils.

Heinie Zimmerman, crossing over.

Oh, what memories!

The World's Oldest Batboy

JOHN B. HOLWAY

At eighty-nine, Hank Le Bost's hair is still red, though a little thinner than it was back in 1915–16, when Casey Stengel "with his big schnozz and guttural voice" called him "Carrot Top" and took him into Ebbets Field to be his mascot.

Hank can still remember Casey, manager Wilbert Robinson, sluggers Zack Wheat and Jake Daubert, and the other Dodgers hoisting beers to celebrate the team's first pennant ever.

"Cuss words galore!" he laughs. "Every third word. Casey and Robinson outdid each other" in purple language.

Le Bost was inducted into the Brooklyn Dodger Hall of Fame three years ago and greets guests wearing his Hall of Fame medallion around his neck like a member of the British Order of the Garter.

With an aquiline nose and just a touch of a Brooklynese accent, Hank's grip is stronger and his tummy tighter than those of most of his visitors. He can throw a frisbee as far as any kid on the block. He ascribes this to squeezing hand grips and pulling extension exercisers 20 minutes every day.

He reads without glasses, sings baritone with his chorale in Lincoln Center, plays bridge, and dances with his 83-year old "lady friend," who "won't marry me because she doesn't want to spoil a good relationship."

Hank was thirteen in 1915. Groceries were delivered to your home by donkey-cart. People rode the old horse-drawn trolley cars, jumping onto running boards alongside the cars and holding on to stanchions. The subway to New York cost five cents.

He remembers walking from his father's candy store on East Parkway and Troy Avenue, past "a wilderness" of vacant lots filled with squatter's shacks and grazing nanny goats, to Bedford Avenue and the brand new Ebbets Field. He hung out at the players' entrance with a gang of other boys, all hoping one of the players would take a shine to him.

At last one day Stengel, then twenty-five and the regular right-fielder, spotted Hank's bright red hair. "Heh, Red, come on in," he said. The Dodgers won that day, and the next time Casey saw him, he brought him in again.

Casey Stengel in 1913

"I became his pet. I was more of a mascot than a batboy."
Like the other players, Casey jealously carried his own bats,
afraid to let anyone else touch them. Each man had two bats,
which he carefully kept in a canvas batbag. "They took good
care of their bats, because they were expensive."

Today's "batboys" didn't appear until the modern-day
dugout bat racks about 1930, Le Bost says.

Hank shagged fly balls, joining other boys in the outfield
for pregame fielding practice. If a ball was out of Casey's
reach, instead of running for it, he called out to Hank, "You
get it, kid."

Hank's other job was as a "manservant" to buy snacks for
Casey and the others.

In 1916 Nathan's famous Coney Island hot dogs went on
sale for the first time in Ebbets Field. "That was their first
stand," Le Bost says. Real Brooklynites swear that they were
the most delicious hot dogs ever cooked—the steaming
franks literally went "pop" with the first bite.

Frankfurters were a nickel, a soft drink a nickel, a schooner of beer a nickel, and knishes two for a nickel. The players
and Robinson would send him into the stands to bring back
provisions for them.

"A good many had big paunchy bellies," he recalls.
"Robinson went up to about 230 pounds. A big belly."

Robinson was the big tipper—he gave the kid two cents.
"The other ball players were each a penny."

But Hank and his friends saved their pennies till the end
of the week. A subway ride was five cents. The movies, or
"nickelodeon," sold two tickets for a nickel, "and if you had
an extra two or three cents in your pocket, you got a big bag
of popcorn."

One day Le Bost got an inspiration: Instead of throwing
the fungoes back to the infield, "maybe I ought to keep one
once in a while. So my mother sewed long pockets in my
baseball uniform on the side of each leg. I'd throw one ball
back and keep one and sold them for 25 cents to the industrial league at Prospect Park."

Casey was a great jokester, then as later, although he had
not yet let the first bird out of his hat at home plate. Le Bost
says Stengel and Robinson competed in playing crude jokes
on each other. One of Casey's favorite props was a "whoopie
cushion," which, when sat on, gave out a loud "brrrrt," like
the old "Bronx cheer."

Today's managers are disciplinarians who remain aloof
from their men. Even Stengel, when he managed the Yankees, always told his hard-drinking charges that they could
drink anywhere except the hotel bar, "because that's where
I drink."

"But in those days the manager was manager in name
only," Le Bost says. "He couldn't tell the players what to do.

They were pals, more or less. Robinson counseled every one
of them, treated them fatherly."

Yet, Hank recalls, "There was less dissension on the
teams then," perhaps because star players made only $3,000
a year, and journeymen made about $2,200.

"Today's players are better athletes and in better condi-
tion," Hank thinks. They can take a 96-mph fastball in the
ribs that would have killed the old-timers. "But I don't think
they throw everything into the game. I think when they
made less money, they were better ballplayers."

Stengel wore a glove that was little bigger than his hand,
compared to today's huge leather claws, says Le Bost. That's
why the old-timers made many more errors.

Today the average big league game draws almost 30,000
people. Ebbets Field then held only 20,000 or so—it was not
yet double-decked—"and many a game they played with
only 1200 people." Bleacher seats cost a quarter, he recalls,
and the grandstand fifty cents.

Boys played marbles, a lost sport today, and wore knick-
ers instead of trousers, and old-fashioned sneakers on their
feet. Older boys wore "high top" shoes—not sneakers—
which were "very snazzy."

Abe Stark was a politician in later years with a large clothing store on Pitkin Avenue. He sold excellent suits, "maybe
85–100 bucks," and rented a sign below the scoreboard in
right field, offering a suit to any player who hit the sign. "But
Abe was a crafty guy," his sign was almost impossible to hit.
"Very seldom did anyone get a suit from Abe Stark."

The Dodgers finished third in 1915 and first in '16. Stengel
batted .237 the first year, .279 the second, and .364 in the
World Series against the Red Sox, which Brooklyn lost, four
games to one.

Casey and Robinson had a falling out when Robbie tried
to catch a ball dropped from an airplane. The "ball" turned
out to be a grapefruit, which splattered all over him, making
him think he'd been killed. He always blamed Casey for the
prank, though Stengel denied it. At any rate, in 1917 Stengel
was gone.

"I was fired," he later told a Senate investigating committee. "I say fired, because there is no doubt I had to leave."

Later Hank tried out for the great semipro team, the
Brooklyn Bushwicks. "They didn't make much money and
had to pass the hat around." Many future major leaguers got
their starts with the Bushwicks. Phil Rizzuto once wore a
Bushwick uniform, and "I think Zack Wheat played with
them. They had a keg of beer at third base. Everyone who hit
a three-bagger or a home run, they had a schooner of beer
waiting for you to take into the dugout. They did things in
those days you couldn't get away with today."

It was rough for Carrigan

Quit
While You're Ahead

JACK KAVANAGH

There were no baseball worlds left for Bill Carrigan to conquer at the end of the 1916 season. His Boston Red Sox were the World's Champions. In fact, in defeating the Brooklyn Dodgers with only the loss of one game, the Red Sox had matched their 1915 World Series triumph, when they also beat the Philadelphia Phillies in five games. Back-to-back championships are a proud way to cap a career, even a short one as the 33-year-old Carrigan's managerial run had been. He took over a dissension-riddled second division Red Sox team in mid-season in 1913, brought it home second in 1914, and then led the team to pennants the next two years. Now he was leaving.

Carrigan's departure was not abrupt. He had told owner Joseph J. Lannin before the 1916 season ended that he would not return. He had spent ten years in the big leagues as Boston's catcher and as a player-manager and he was ready to close off the athletic chapter of his life. Bill Carrigan was a natural athlete who had played two years of football at Holy Cross under the legendary Frank Cavanaugh. Later dubbed the "Iron Major" for World War One heroics, Cavanaugh is a college football Hall of Fame member as a coach. Like Knute Rockne, he was played in a biographical movie by Pat O'Brien. In baseball, Carrigan's Holy Cross coach was Tommy McCarthy, whose 1946 election to the Baseball Hall of Fame raised eyebrows that haven't been lowered yet.

Carrigan was signed by the Red Sox after his sophomore year at Holy Cross, and after a season with Toronto in the International League, he joined Boston in 1906. He was a clever handler of pitchers, and he hit a respectable .257 for his ten-year career at a time when a catcher was not expected to hit for a high average. His final game as a player was the fourth contest of the 1916 Series. It was his only appearance against the Dodgers that fall, and he made it memorable with two hits while catching Hub Leonard's 6-2 victory.

When the Red Sox played their final regular season game, Carrigan stepped out on the field and waved a farewell to the fans. Carrigan had been born in Lewiston, Maine, and he was ready to return to his home town and start a new career. Back in Lewiston, the former Beulah Bartlett, and the family that would grow to include Bill, Jr. and his two sisters, welcomed the idea of a year 'round father.

Carrigan had saved a good share of his ballplayer's salary and World Series money and was ready to invest in a business career. He went from managing a major league ballclub to managing a bank, and he also branched out as owner of a string of movie houses across the state. He had a magic touch, getting in on the growing craze for silent flickers as Chaplin, Fairbanks and Pickford became marquee names outside his theaters. His banking career was more sedate but very successful.

Despite his success both in and out of the game, It's inevitable that Carrigan is defined for most people by his relationship with Babe Ruth. Carrigan was the Babe's first major league manager, and much of what we know about his personality comes from the accounts of Babe Ruth's early years with Boston.

Bill Carrigan had replaced Red Sox manager Jake Stahl in 1913, after the contentious Stahl had allowed the 1912 champions to disintegrate into cantankerous factions. He was the Red Sox manager when the 19-year-old George Herman Ruth was delivered from Baltimore in mid-season. Actually, Bill Carrigan was none too pleased to have the teenage parolee from a boys training school assigned to him. Ruth, a young giant, combined the callowness of youth with an almost total lack of discipline. He needed strong and steady handling. Bill Carrigan supplied it, if reluctantly. The

manager was already called "Rough" by his teammates for his willingness to mix it up whenever necessary. As is usual with those who have the physique to back up a squared-jawed determination, the squat, five foot six inch, 175 pound Carrigan rarely had to lift his fists to quell a disturbance.

Ruth arrived with another outstanding pitching prospect, Ernie Shore. Of the two, Shore filled Carrigan's needs the best. Unlike Ruth, he was righthanded, and a gap in the Red Sox staff had existed since Smoky Joe Wood's strong right arm had gone lame two years before. Wood, a 34-game winner in 1912, would never regain his blazing fastball. With Carrigan's deft handling, he learned to pitch craftily and win in certain spots. But the Boston staff was led in 1914 by 20-game winner Ray Collins and Hub "Dutch" Leonard, who won 19. Both were lefties, and what Carrigan and the Sox needed was a strong young right arm.

Carrigan did put Ruth to work as soon as he had climbed off the train from Baltimore, putting him on the mound that very afternoon and catching him himself. The Babe pitched impressively until he weakened in the seventh inning, when he left with the game tied. After Duffy Lewis drove in a go-ahead run pinch-hitting for Ruth, Leonard came in to pitch two scoreless innings of relief and preserve the Babe's first big league win. However, Carrigan rarely used the Babe at all after that, and later in the season the big kid was sent down to Providence. Years later, in an interview for Robert W. Creamer's outstanding biography, *Babe: The Legend Comes To Life*, Carrigan told the author, "I've read many times that Ruth was sent down for more seasoning, but that's not true. He was already a finished pitcher, good enough for us or anybody else. But we were out of our pennant race and Lannin [who also owned the Providence Grays of the International League] to win theirs."

Ernie Shore provided a late-in-life appreciation of Bill Carrigan, telling the author and oral historian Donald Honig, "Bill Carrigan was the tops. Best manager in the world. He was close to his players, and he had their respect. I never heard a man speak ill of him."

Babe Ruth chafed at Carrigan's reluctance to use him as a rookie or give him a starting role in the 1915 World Series, but he made the most of his upgraded role in 1916. After his sensational 14-inning defeat of Brooklyn in the 1916 World Series, hold the Dodgers scoreless for the final 13 innings, the Babe shouted to Carrigan, "I told you a year ago I could take care of those National League bums and you never gave me a chance." Nonetheless, in later years the Babe always rated Bill Carrigan as his favorite manager.

Carrigan has been faulted for not capitalizing on Ruth's hitting ability. It wasn't until after Ed Barrow had taken over the Red Sox in 1918 that the Babe began appearing in the outfield when he was not on the mound. There were sound reasons why Bill Carrigan was satisfied to let well enough alone and use Babe Ruth strictly as a pitcher. Until he was sold by the Red Sox after the 1915 season, Tris Speaker had combined with Duffy Lewis and Harry Hooper to form an outfield some historians still contend was the best of all time. Even after the great Speaker left, the pitching staff needed a full time Babe Ruth more than the team needed a new outfielder. The Babe had become the best lefthanded pitcher in the league, winning 23 games in 1916 and leading the league with a 1.25 ERA.

Although Ruth, when he connected, sent awesome drives to distant parts of ballparks, he was an inconsistent hitter and a disappointment as a pinch hitter. Carrigan sent the Babe to bat thirty times as a pinch hitter, but got only five hits for a .167 average. Overall, however, the Babe hatted .286 with seven home runs while pitching for Carrigan. Nonetheless, the conservative Bill Carrigan always had the Babe bat ninth, the pitcher's traditional place in the lineup.

Carrigan contributed positively to the emerging career of the ebullient youth whose self-confidence was a danger to team harmony. The veteran players were shocked by a rookie who insisted he was entitled to a turn at bat in pre-game practice. Once they sawed the Babe's bats in half. However, Carrigan smoothed the way to acceptance and Ruth's superior skills convinced his teammates he belonged wherever he insisted he did.

The story of Bill Carrigan, the man who was smart enough to retire when he was at the top, unfortunately has a conclusion as down-sided as the triumphant 1916 departure was upbeat. Soon after Carrigan's retirement, Joseph Lannin sold the Red Sox to theatrical entrepreneur Harry Frazee. In a few years Frazee had destroyed the franchise by selling Babe Ruth to the New York Yankees in 1920. Other Red Sox stars were shipped to New York City, and Boston dropped into the cellar. They finished last—except for one heady elevator ride to seventh place—every year from 1922 to 1926.

The owner of the shattered franchise left behind by Frazee was John Quinn, who knew baseball but was broke. He appealed to Bill Carrigan to return and turn Fenway Park into Camelot once again. Still a young man in his early forties, comfortably well off and far too idle to suit his need for challenges, Carrigan let himself be talked into a two-year contract. Alas, the magic was gone. Babe Ruth was gone. Baseball had changed. Ruth's booming bat had encouraged a new style of play, and Carrigan simply didn't have the players to meet the challenge.

It was 1927, and in New York, the Babe, along with players who had been in school when Carrigan rode high with the Red Sox, was the most fearsome member of the Yankees "Murderers Row." The Red Sox finished last in 1927 and 1928. Carrigan stayed for one last try in 1929, which was also a bad year for bankers. Again, the Red Sox finished in the cellar, and Bill Carrigan retired again to small town life in Lewiston. He was a popular local figure, often called on to speak at sports gatherings. He always told them about 1916, the year he led the Red Sox to a second consecutive World Championship. If he had any advice, it must have been, "quit while you're ahead."

Joe DeMaggio?

The Magnificent Yankee

CARL LUNDQUIST

He was and is the Magnificent Yankee, the greatest player these believing eyes have seen in fifty-seven years as a privileged observer of major league baseball.

And it is an irony that won't quit that "the lanky Yankee with the wide stride" began life in professional baseball as Joe DiMaggio because a San Francisco sportswriter, who should forever remain anonymous, erroneously immortalized the proud old DeMaggio family by misspelling the name when he was covering older brother Vince as an outfielder for the Pacific Coast League Seals.

The error stuck, and the three ball-playing brothers christened Vincenzo, Giuseppe, and Dominic were known forever as DiMaggios and not by the proper heritage of their father, Giuseppe (Joseph) DeMaggio, Sr., a career fisherman.

In this commemoration of the golden anniversary of one of baseball's most momentous seasons, the lasting question that year in every American League dugout was who could stop Joe DiMaggio?

It was his greatest year by nearly every measurement in a Yankee career that stretched from 1936 through 1951, with three seasons departed from the diamond as he wore World War II khakis, 1943–45.

Mark it indelibly, the season of 1941 produced what many seasoned observers declare to be the number one all-time individual batting mark, that 56-game hitting streak of the Yankee Clipper. Still, it was not all that he had sought to achieve because he failed in his quest for a third straight American League batting championship.

And in that context is it not fair to reminisce about how in the world the very last of baseball's .400 hitters could be deprived of the annual award to the league's "Most Valuable Player"? The baseball writers of America that season had to choose between Joltin' Joe, 56 in a row, or Thumpin' Theodore, who batted .406 but had to settle for second place in the MVP reckonings. Williams in his third season as a Red Socker, also led the league in home runs with 37, but DiMaggio outnumbered him in runs batted in 125 to 120.

DiMag goes down to get hit number 43.

DiMaggio had 30 homers among his 193 hits, Williams wound up with 185 hits, but gained the batting title by having considerably fewer times at bat: 456 to 541 for DiMaggio.

That batting title which eluded the Yankee outfielder would have enabled him to be the first three-time champ since Ty Cobb of the Tigers had three in a row from 1917 through 1919 after he laid in another mark that is not likely ever to be matched, his nine straight from 1907 through 1915. Tris Speaker of the Indians muscled in for one season, winning the title in 1916, despoiling what would have become an unsurpassable string of thirteen in a row.

DiMaggio, in fact, had to settle for third place in the AL batting race for that season. His highly respectable mark of .357 was topped also by Cecil Travis of Washington, who was two points higher at .359.

It is perhaps the greatest lure of the national pastime to be free to delve into statistical probabilities, so here now comes a compulsion to wonder about what might have been. First there was the combined effort of four Cleveland players who loaded up to derail DiMaggio in a night game on July 14 before 67,468 fans, the largest crowd that had yet been assembled in the city's huge lake-front stadium.

The end did not come easily. Lefty Al Smith, who had more luck than guile, managed to retire DiMaggio twice because third baseman Ken Keltner made successive backhanded stops of drives that appeared to be sure hits. Going back and being off balance, he somehow managed to throw Joe out both times. Smith complicated matters by walking Joe on his third appearance.

Opportunity was knocking when Jim Bagby, a righthander, was on the hill to face Joe in his final at bat of the streak. The bases were loaded and Joe, always at his best when there was a chance to drive in runs, hit a drive cleanly to shortstop Lou Boudreau. Just as Lou reached for it, the ball took an errant hop and he had to reach for it with his bare hand. Boudreau, noting later that "it stung like hell," made an instant throw and ended it all for the jolter.

Now it is numbers time and you can try these on for size. First, there was that new 56, an all-time major league mark. Backward in time try on number 61, an all-time Pacific Coast League mark that had been set by a rookie outfielder—yes, it was Joe—who ran up that streak with San Francisco in 1933. Finally, and now it gets murky as we enter the Twilight Zone, how about number 73? It did not quite happen and brings to mind the sad rhyme of John Greenleaf Whittier, who penned them in his epic poem "Maud Muller." In another context, connoting another near-miss he wrote: "Of all sad words of tongue or pen, the saddest are these, *it might have been.*"

Had it not been for the combined efforts of that Cleveland quartet, DiMaggio might have gone on to 73 consecutive games, surpassing every streak known to man in major or minor key. The all-time record of 69 still stands belonging, probably forever, to Joe Wilhoit of the 1919 Wichita, Kansas, team in the Western League.

Moving along as though he had been halted briefly at a roadblock, DiMaggio ran up another streak of 16 that ended on August 3 right at home in Yankee Stadium, this time not with a whimper but with a bang, or was it a bang-bang against the lowly St. Louis Browns? On that day in a doubleheader, Joe went 0-for-8, being blanked in the opener by knuckleball pitcher John Niggeling, and by the fastballs of Bob Harris in the second game.

There is a necessity in recounting this notable year to realize that America was less than a semester away from total involvement in World War II. The comparison is valid, even now, as there is some concern that all sports become true trivia when measured against the new world conflict in the Persian Gulf.

And war was on the minds of this scrivener in 1941 when toiling in a double role as a wire editor and sportswriter for the worldwide news-gathering minions of the United Press. A summer vacation visit to the San Francisco UP offices put the issue clearly into focus. Don Caswell, later to become a war correspondent, was on duty there and questioned what seemed to be the daily necessity of breaking into war stories in Europe with the news that DiMaggio had gone yet another day in his streak.

"The DiMaggio streak is the bore of the year," said scoffer Caswell, noting that except for sports nuts, no one really cared.

How could the man say such a thing, in San Francisco, of all places? A test case was required and both writers emerged from the shop to ask the first man on the street about DiMaggio. A dapper little fellow in a straw hat was encountered with the question "How did Joe do today?"

"Joe got 2-for-4, and the Yankees beat the White Sox, 5 to 4," was the instant response. He also noted that he had never been to a ballgame in his life.

That night in Joe DiMaggio's almost brand new restaurant on Fisherman's Wharf, the food was especially tasty and the band leader filled in all the details for late arrivals about Joe's latest episode.

Sadly, Caswell was right about the war and its impact on every American, and after another season DiMaggio hung up his baseball flannels, donned GI livery, and was in military service for three full seasons, 1943 through 1945.

DiMaggio, who will be feted frequently in this anniversary year, was given a standing ovation at the annual dinner of the New York Baseball Writers when he was presented with a crystal trophy emblematic of his lifelong achievements in baseball.

The Waterford Vase, honoring Joe on the fiftieth anniversary year of his streak, was especially meaningful as he noted in his acceptance remarks that other priceless trophies in his collection had been destroyed in the family home on San Francisco's North Beach in the earthquake that smashed the area during the 1989 World Series.

Someone noted that since it was in the record books as a game of major consequence, Joe's streak should be at 57, because he got a hit in the All-Star game at Detroit that year in the midst of his league streak.

"No way," he said. "That was just an exhibition. But we beat the National League, didn't we?"

DiMaggio also remembered that the game that ended his streak was a 4–3 Yankee victory, a major consolation with the team in a drive for the American League pennant, which it eventually won. And the Indians, in second place, were the team they had to beat.

Regarding speculation that he might have extended his record by those 16 additional games had he not been stopped, DiMaggio said that was a hypothetical situation that would have involved vastly different circumstances.

"There would have been additional pressure on me and on every team trying to stop me," he said. "No one could know how it might have turned out. Maybe I was more at ease again after the streak was over."

There were numerous times during the streak when he was not in any way at ease.

Consider the case of the stolen bat. He recalled to Herb Goren, long-time network writer of sports scripts for CBS and ABC, and once the "Old Scout," writing under that name for the *New York Sun*, that this was a major dilemma.

"It wasn't just any bat," he declared. "This was a very special bat."

He ordered the bats by the dozen, Louisville Sluggers from Hillerich & Bradsby. And the one he prized the most disappeared before streak game 40.

When he was up for the first time, he realized that his number 1 bat was not in the rack. The Yankees were in

Washington, playing a doubleheader, and later an usher confided that he had seen a youngster "fooling around the bat rack."

"I had worked on that bat," he said. "You pick out one from the new batch that feels just right and dip it in olive oil, rub it down with resin, flame treat it for hardening. When it got dry, I'd sandpaper it. But it was gone and I had to use my backup bat. Well I got hits in both games, so it turned out all right."

Eventually, with no questions asked, a youth from Newark, New Jersey, returned the bat, and Joe, grateful to have it back, donated his substitute bat to the United Service Organization (USO), where it was sold for $1,600 for war benefit funds.

There were pitchers who gave him more trouble than the lad who pilfered the bat.

During the day-to-day pressure that built up during the 56-game run, DiMaggio's biggest problems involved pitchers who today are mere obscurities on yellowing old scorecards—not Hall of Famers like Bobby Feller. He rapped Bullet Bob for three hits, two of them doubles in the two games they were matched against each other.

Instead, take a look at moundsmen like Eldon Auker, Dick Newsome, Charley Muncrief, and Johnny Babich, hurlers whose names were not exactly household words, even in their own kitchens.

Auker, a Browns pitcher whose deliveries came in underhand or side-arm, previously had gained a measure of fame as an all-conference halfback for the Kansas State Wildcats, 1929–31. But he was the first to give Joe Trouble. In game six Joe was 0-for-3 until the eighth inning, when he finally eked out a single. Again in game 38 it was tension time as DiMaggio had to extend things with another eighth-inning final turn at bat. He hit the first pitch for a double, noting that the Kansas submarine server gave him trouble because he threw a lot of bad pitches, and it was difficult to see where they were coming from.

It was an entirely different kind of delivery that was troublesome in game nine, where Red Sox pitcher Dick Newsome threw only fastballs. Seemingly everybody but Joe was connecting safely that day in a game that ended in a 9–9 tie, with all records remaining on the books. He recalled that Newsome always was tough for him to hit, though under normal circumstances Joe devoured fastballs. And he hit one of them safely to prolong the streak.

A fellow can't get revenge before the fact, but it was an item worth remembering that DiMaggio pounded Cleveland pitcher Bagby for a home run for his hit in game 28 of the streak. He remarked about that blast when he was pained to admit that Bagby and Smith had collared him in game 57.

Two better-than-average pitchers also were troublesome. The veteran Mel Harder of the Indians stopped him until the eighth inning of the eighteenth game, when Joe drilled a single past the troublesome third-sacker Keltner. It was a matter of sportsmanship that was notable for

Elden Auker submarines it.

Browns pitcher Bob Muncrief in the final inning of the thirty-seventh game. Muncrief had stopped Joe in the three previous times at bat and was on the verge of walking him when he threw a hard one into the strike zone that DiMag conked for a record-extending single.

"I could not have walked Joe," Muncrief commented. "A walk would not have been fair to him or to me. I tried to get him out with a good pitch and he hit it. He's the greatest player I've ever seen."

Not all of the pitching opponents were so noble. Johnny Babich, who was described as a "ham and egg" pitcher for the Athletics, but who had gained a reputation for pitching well against the Yankees, commented to assembled scribes that he was going to stop DiMaggio. That was before the fortieth game of the streak in Philadelphia. With no strategic reason to do so, he walked the slugger on four pitches in his first at bat. Up again in the fourth, the count was 3–0 when Joe got testy.

"The next pitch was outside, but I reached out and lined it between Johnny's legs for a clean hit."

Joe swore he had no intent to maim Babich but noted when he made his turn at first that old John was as white as a sheet. He also used the incident to credit manager Joe McCarthy for going against standard strategy.

"McCarthy was great to me," he said. "He let me hit the 3–0 pitch quite a few times, but that's the one I remember the best."

Day after day during the prolonged stretch from May 15 through July 16, DiMaggio stepped over past achievers, who at one time had held the mark for consecutive games. The biggie was the major league mark of 44, untouched since 1897, when Willie Keeler, the fabled place hitter for the Baltimore Orioles of the National League, set the record.

En route Joe swept by George Sisler's American League total of 41, set with the Browns in 1922. Prior to that Ty Cobb had 40 in a row in 1911 and in 1938. George McQuinn of the Browns, later to become a Yankee teammate, did 34 straight. Each level was duly noted in the chronicles of the DiMaggio consecutive run, and to put that 56 total into final focus, one needs to remember that the top National League total is still Keeler's 44, equaled in 1978 by Pete Rose, one more accomplishment that will not bring him into the Hall of Fame. Rose topped the previous modern National League mark, held by Tommy Holmes, who went 37 straight with the 1945 Boston Braves.

Because of the intensity of the competition for MVP honors in that golden year of yore, it needs to be noted that although DiMaggio banged out a hit in the All-Star Game, it was Williams who stole the show. In the bottom of the ninth with two men aboard, Ted crashed a homer over the stadium roof to give the American League a 7–5 triumph.

Significant to this Kansas-born observer, who toiled in newspaper shops in Kansas City for a decade before moving to New York, was the fact that four of DiMaggio's teammates

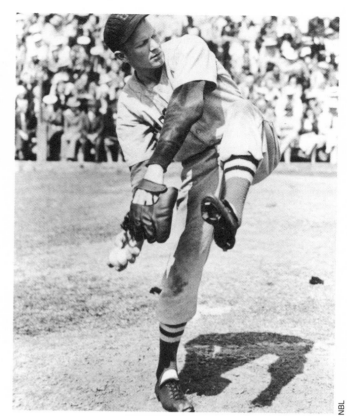

Dick Newsome

in his record-breaking season had been stars for the Kansas City blues, the Yankees' top farm club in the American Association the previous season.

In fact, Johnny Sturm, the rookie who became a regular at first base, had a streak going ahead of DiMaggio and was singled out by the media for his day-to-day connections which reached 12 in a row in a game at Washington that was subsequently rained out. And with the rainout went Sturm's streak; he was hitless the next day. And at that time the scribes picked up on DiMaggio, who heretofore had been largely ignored—the rookie was making the news.

The other ex-Blues were pitcher Ernie Bonham, who had a winning 9–6 season; shortstop Phil Rizzuto, who replaced Frank Crosetti as a regular; and Jerry Priddy, who shared second base duties with Joe Gordon. All were friends when they toiled in the dark navy livery of the Blues. It was the special privilege of this lifetime member of the Baseball Writers to nominate Rizzuto for the distinguished long and meritorious service award at the New York dinner a year before, inasmuch as their friendship extended beyond all others in the New York chapter, beginning at old Muehlebach Field in Kansas City.

As the Frank Sinatra song goes, despite the war clouds of 1941, "It Was a Very Good Year."

Sisyphus had nothing on Old Mose

300 for Lefty

PAUL DOHERTY

When the 1941 season opened, Lefty Grove needed seven wins to reach the 300 level, which had been attained by only eleven pitchers in the major leagues going all the way back to 1888.

It was a tough battle for a forty-one-year old pitcher.

In spring training 1941 Grove was kept idle by cold weather and an injury to his pitching hand. He did not appear in a game until April 6 in Birmingham, where he pitched three innings.

When the 1941 regular season opened, Bob Grove became a weekend pitcher and made his first start April 18, Boston's third game. He pitched seven innings and was losing, 2–1, when Ted Williams pinch-hit for him. The Sox went on to win, but Lefty didn't get the victory.

He lost a start in late April due to cold weather.

Grove won the penultimate Number 299 against the last-place A's July 3 at home. Grove would have won his 300th game two or three years earlier, but he had spent too many years in the minor leagues, winning 108 games in 1920–24, back when minor-league clubs were not subject to the major-league draft. His owner, Jack Dunn of Baltimore in the International League, paid good salaries to keep his best players as he managed the Orioles to seven consecutive pennants, 1919–25. It two of these minor-league years had been spent in the majors, Lefty might have gained 50 more victories.

During that time he defeated the Yankees twice in exhibitions. He was finally sold to the Philadelphia Athletics for $100,600—the $600 was thrown in to break the previous record of $100,000, which the Yankees had paid the Red Sox for Babe Ruth.

He almost won Number 300 in Detroit, losing a six-hitter to the Tigers, 2–0.

A week later another veteran pitcher, Chicago's Ted Lyons, beat him in ten innings, 4–3.

On Friday, July 25, the Red Sox were home, and the Boston Globe headline read:

"Third Time Won't Fail,"
Grove Vows In 300 Quest

It was Ladies' Day, and 6,000 women came out to see him pitch. The game was a thriller. Cleveland took a 4–0 lead with three runs in the third on five hits in a row. Slow baserunning stopped the Indians from adding more runs, but it looked bad for Lefty.

The Red Sox scored two runs in the fourth. In the fifth, Williams' 19th homer, with a man on, tied the score at 4–4.

Grove settled down and shut out Cleveland for the next three innings. But the Tribe went ahead in the seventh when Lou Boudreau homered. Gee Walker tripled and scored when Jim Tabor at third base couldn't handle the throw from the outfield. The Indians led, 6–4.

In the seventh Williams walked and Tabor homered to tie the score again, 6–6. Grove almost won the game himself. After catcher Johnny Peacock singled, Old Man Mose doubled, but Peacock was caught at the plate trying to score.

Into the eighth inning, with high humidity and 90-degree heat, went the worn-out veteran. The Indians were helpless in the eighth, for Grove kept them off the bases.

In the bottom of the eighth, leadoff man Dom DiMaggio and manager Joe Cronin walked. Williams came up with a chance to give the Sox the lead, but he fouled out to third.

The next batter was Jimmie Foxx, the man Lefty, in the in the eighth, for Grove kept them off the bases.

In the bottom of the eighth, leadoff man Dom DiMaggio and manager Joe Cronin walked. Williams came up with a chance to give the Sox the lead, but he fouled out to third.

The next batter was Jimmie Foxx, the man Lefty, in the dugout, was hoping would come up in such a situation. His booming bat had won many a game for Grove in the past, both in Philadelphia's great championship years, 1929–31, and in Boston. This day, however, Foxx's bat had been quiet; he had walked twice and fouled out. But Jimmie hit a tremendous drive off the center-field wall for a triple to make it 9–6. Tabor then hit his second successive homer for a final score of 10–6.

Grove had thrown almost 120 pitches. He said later he had nothing on the ball, that his curve was belted all around and was useless in the last two innings, when all he had was his fastball.

Peacock would agree that Lefty may not have had good stuff, but he had control: the Indians got only a solitary base on balls.

In the ninth, Grove got pinch-hitters Rollie Helmsley (.240) and Beau Bell (.192). Next was leadoff man Boudreau

(.257), who already had a homer and two singles for the day. But Lou flied out to DiMaggio, and Grove had won his 300th.

As Lefty walked off the mound, fans rushed out and surrounded him. Men hugged him and patted him on the back (no mention of what the lady fans did). The crowd on the field got bigger by the second, and it took a squad of police to make a path for Lefty.

Inside the clubhouse the reporters and photographers were waiting. Grove got on the scales and found he had lost eight pounds during the game.

Lefty tried seven more times to win number 301 with no success. On August 27 he pulled a muscle pitching to the leadoff man and was out for a month.

On the final day of the season Grove returned for one more attempt, in Philadelphia, the scene of his great glories a decade earlier. He was knocked out in the first inning and never pitched in the major leagues again.

THE 300TH WIN
JUNE 25, 1941

Boston	ab	r	h	Cleveland	ab	r	h
DiMaggio, cf	4	1	0	Boudreau, ss	5	2	3
Finney, rf	4	1	1	Rosenthal, cf	4	1	1
Cronin, ss	4	2	0	Walker, lf	4	1	2
L. Newsome, ss	0	0	0	Heath, rf	4	2	2
Williams, lf	3	3	2	Keltner, 3b	4	0	2
Spencer, lf	0	0	0	Troskey, 1b	2	0	1
Foxx, 1b	3	1	1	Mack, 2b	1	0	0
Tabor, 3b	4	2	3	Grimes, 2b-1b	4	0	0
Doerr, 2b	5	0	0	Desaultels, c	3	0	1
Peacock, c	3	0	2	*a.* Hemsley	1	0	0
Grove, p	4	0	1	Krakauskas, p	1	0	0
Harder, p	1	0	0		34	10	10
Milnar, p	0	0	0	*b.* Bell	1	0	0
					36	6	12

Bos 000 220 24x - 10 10   Cle 013 000 200 - 6 12

a batted for Desautels in 9th, b batted for Milnar in 9th
rbi - Boudreau, Walker, Heath, Keltner, Grimes, Tabor 4, Williams 2, Foxx 2, Peacock
Two base hits - Keltner 2, Boudreau, Grove, Three base hits Walker, Foxx, HR - Boudreau, Tabor 2, Williams, SB - Boudreau, Heath, Sacr - Finney
LOB - Cleveland 4, Boston 2
BB - off Krakauskas 4, Harder 2, Milnar 2, Grove 1
SO - by Krakauskas 3, Harder 1, Milnar 1, Grove 6
Hits - off Krakauskas 1 in 3 inn. (pitched to 4 in 4th, none out)
Harder 6 in 3 2/3 inn., Milnar 3 in 1 1/3
LP - Milnar
Umpires - McGowan Quinn, Grieve
Time - 2 h., 27 m.
Attendance (estimated) - 10,000 paid (6,000 ladies)

GROVE'S GAME-BY-GAME RECORD 1941

No.	Date	Where	Score			IP	H	SO	W/L	R'crd
	Apr 18	Phi	Bos 3	Phi 2		7	2	2	-	0–0
	Apr 29	Det	Det 5	Bos 3		3	7	3	L	0–1
294	May 4	StL	Bos 11	StL 4		9*	8	3	W	1–1
295	May 12	Bos	Bos 11	StL 4		9*	10	4	W	2–1
	May 18	Bos	Det 6	Bos 5	(11)	7	8	1	–	2–1
296	May 25	NY	Bos 10	NY 3		9*	7	1	W	3–1
	June 1	Det	Bos 7	Det 6		6.1	11	2	-	3–1
297	June 8	Chi	Bos 5	Chi 3		10*	8	7	W	4–1
	June 15	Bos	Bos 8	Chi 6		3.2	5	3	-	4–1
	June 21	Bos	StL 13	Bos 9		1.2	5	0	L	4–2
298	June 25	Bos	Bos 7	Cle 2		9*	7	5	W	5–2
299	July 3	Phi	Bos 5	Phi 2		9*	10	2	W	6–2
	July 11	Det	Det 2	Bos 0		8*	6	4	L	6–3
	July 18	Chi	Chi 4	Bos 3		10*	7	1	L	6–4
300	July 25	Bos	Bos 10	Cle 6		9*	12	6	W	7–4
	Aug 2	Bos	Det 6	Bos 5		9*	8	2	L	7–5
	Aug 9	Bos	Was 8	Bos 6		7	16	2	-	7–5
	Aug 16	Was	Bos 8	Was 6		6	9	6	-	7–5
	Aug 20	StL	StL 11	Bos 9		0.2	4	0	L	7–6
	Aug 27	Det	Det 6	Bos 3		0.1	0	0	-	7–6
	Sep 28	Phi	Phi 7	Bos 18		1	4	0	L	7–7

*Complete games.
August 27 Grove pulled a muscle in his side pitching to Stainback, leadoff batter.
Grove started all 21 games.

"Durocher put a little fire under me, to tell you the truth"

Whit Wyatt — The Dodgers' 1941 Ace

THOMAS LILEY

John Whitlow Wyatt, the Brooklyn Dodgers' top pitcher in the early 1940s, almost didn't make it to the National League. After nine unsuccessful years in the American League with Detroit, Chicago, and Cleveland, the big righthander was ready to leave baseball for his farm in Buchanan, Georgia.

Henry Bendinger, owner of the old Milwaukee Brewers, talked Wyatt into giving the game one more chance with an offer of 15 percent of the purchase price if Wyatt were sold to a major league club at the end of that 1938 season. Wyatt took a straight contract of $700 a month instead, a decision that cost him $6,000. He threw 9 shutouts, led the American Association in strikeouts, and sported a 23–7 record. Two teams were interested in him—the Boston Braves and the Brooklyn Dodgers—and, on Bendinger's advice that Babe Ruth would be the Dodgers' manager, Wyatt chose Brooklyn, who paid $40,000 and three players for him.

Ruth, of course, didn't manage the Dodgers. Wyatt's new manager was Leo Durocher, who, Wyatt says, "could think quicker than anybody I ever saw….Durocher put a little fire under me, to tell you the truth. To be frank, he taught me to be a little mean as a pitcher. I'd come in and find two or three hundred dollars on top of my locker after knocking somebody down."

Wyatt and the Dodgers improved each year: Wyatt's victories increased from 8 in 1939 to 15 in 1940 and 22 in 1941 and the team moved from third to second and, finally in 1941, the Dodgers claimed their first pennant since 1920. The righthander matched his teammate Kirby Higbe for the most wins that championship season with 22; he led in shutouts (7) and was second in complete games (23), strikeouts (176), and earned run average (2.34). He was third in the MVP voting behind fellow Dodgers Dolph Camilli and Pete Reiser, the first time that players from the same club

Whitlow Wyatt

Kirby Higbe

Dolph Camilli

were the top three vote-getters for the award. Wyatt also was selected to start the All-Star Game for the National League against his former teammate, Bob Feller.

Wyatt remembers the 1941 Dodgers well. "I don't think you could ever get a first baseman any better than Camilli. He was a great hitter and the best fielding first baseman I ever saw. [Pete] Coscarart [at second] was as good a fielder as [Billy] Herman, but he wasn't as good a hitter. Herman would hit and run. He could do so many things. We wanted Herman to get to second base; [from there] he'd see the catcher give two signs and he'd have the pitches. He would step left foot over right to show the curveball or right foot out for the fastball. We knew all the signs that year—Billy Herman was the smartest ballplayer I ever saw. Camilli was the big RBI man on the club… Lavagetto was a pretty good hitter… and Dixie Walker wasn't bad, either!"

The pitching staff had a strong Southern flavor, with Wyatt and Hugh Casey from Georgia and Higbe from South Carolina. "Casey would as soon hit you between the eyes as anything. We were real good friends. Of all the people you would not think would kill himself. He had financial problems and he was a pretty good drinker—he drank that hard stuff. But he was a good-hearted fellow.

"Higbe had a better curveball. He should have been a great pitcher, but there were a lot of other things that entered into it, too. He didn't take too good care of himself. And he wasn't a 'fine' pitcher. To be a good pitcher, you have to be able to throw a strike anytime you want to on any pitch you've got. Higbe, when he got ahead of a hitter, he'd let up.

"I was just the opposite. I believe at times I could throw a strike any time. I didn't want to throw one every time, but if I got behind a hitter I could.

"Roscoe McGowen (of *The New York Times*), said that I threw high and tight better than anybody. I got lefthanders out because I pitched outside—that was my alley. I could really hit that corner. I had a slider, which was an unusual pitch at that time. My fastball would rise, and hitters would get under it all the time. The hitters who punched the ball gave me the most trouble, hitters like Lonnie Frey and Stan

Hack. (But) I liked the hitters who swung hard—I could fool them.

Perhaps the turning point of the season was the Dodgers' series at St. Louis in September. "We went in there to play and I believe we were one-and-a-half games ahead of the Cardinals. We had a meeting and Durocher says, 'Whit, how do you feel?'

"I said, 'Well, I've had two days rest. I feel that if I had another day's rest it would help me.' Fitzsimmons pitched and won, and I kidded him about that game. I told him 'You didn't pitch that game today—you talked your way through that game.' Boy, he was a competitor if there ever was one.

"I started [on the thirteenth against Mort Cooper] and I didn't have anything. I just fiddled around and I made good pitches, but I didn't have good stuff. I thought, 'Gosh, I won't last long in this game.' I was that kind of pitcher, though; if you beat me, you had to beat me in the first two or three innings, 'cause if I ever went past that number, brother, I'd pitch nine innings. I believe in 1941 I pitched 23 complete games.

"In about the fourth inning [the fifth, actually] somebody [Creepy Crespi] hit a double off of me and another Cardinal hit a ball to the shortstop and Pee Wee [Reese] fielded the ball but the fellow on second base tried to go to third. Pee Wee threw the ball away and the ball lacked about that much of going into the dugout, which would have been an automatic run. Now I had two men on base and nobody out.

"For some reason or other, my stuff just came to me, just like that. I struck out the catcher, Gus Mancuso, and then I struck out the pitcher, Mort Cooper. Then the third baseman came up, a lefthanded hitter, kind of a pesky hitter [Jimmy Brown]. I threw him a slow curve and he grounded out to first base."

Pounding the table for emphasis, Wyatt continued: "I got out of that inning without a run and I had the *most stuff* in a ballgame I ever had in my life after that. A pitcher makes a lot of mistakes and he still gets your men out, but they're still mistakes. That day I don't believe I made a mistake in that ballgame.

"Enos Slaughter didn't play that day. He came up to pinch-hit in the ninth inning. Durocher walked out of the dugout and says, 'You know this fellow can hurt you, don't you?' Well, I didn't say anything; I knew he wasn't going to hit me *that* day. I threw three fastballs right by him and struck him out and got out of that game and beat 'em 1–0. I think that was the best game I ever pitched in my life."

Twelve days later Wyatt beat the Boston Braves 6–0 to clinch Brooklyn's first championship in twenty-one years.

A Plea Grows in Brooklyn—

"Please Don't Let Them Knock Me Off This Roof!"

BOB RULAND

The other day John Holway asked me how it came to be that I happened to be on that Flatbush rooftop on Sunday, October 5, 1941.

This is a good question, seeing as how it was well known to one and all that at that time I was a fourteen-year-old Giants' fan who did not generally care to mingle with Yankee or Dodger fans. It was my opinion that the former group are snobs while the latter seem to be somewhat boisterous.

Well, anyway, the answer is that my father was a NYPD cop who got assigned to guard this roof in back of Bedford Avenue. Since it overlooked Ebbets Field and a World Series was in progress, the landlord did not wish to have a large number of freeloaders congregate thereupon, thus causing it to cave in and create a variety of problems. Therefore only tenants of this four-story walkup were permitted to gain access thereto. Naturally, in my own personal case I enjoyed a special status.

When we arrived I quickly came to realize that the big scoreboard in right-center blocked much of the view. One had to choose between the two ends of the building. The one on the right revealed only left and center fields. I decided to take up a position to the left where I could see down the right field line, including home plate.

Shortly after I sat down in back of this low parapet, I was joined by two occupants of the fourth-floor rear. One was a tall thin fellow with a large Adam's apple who wore a flat peecap. The other guy was short and fat and appeared not to have shaved for several days. He wore a derby with a dent. I never learned their names.

As the fourth game of this series got ready to start, I could tell from the manner in which they spoke that they were Dodger fans of long standing. I therefore considered it wise to conceal my true identity. So I told them I was from St. Louis and was rooting for the Browns. This resulted in some very mournful looks. It was some years later that I confessed this venial sin to the SABR priest, Father Beirne, who for penance instructs me to apologize to Bill Borst and Ron Gabriel for this transgression. I now do so.

Anyway, they seemed to be pretty agreeable folks who told many Brooklyn stories, including one about how they watched from this very roof in 1920 when the Clevelands clobbered the Robins. It seemed that was what the local fans called them in those days on account of the manager's name was Wilbert Robinson.

I will not dwell at any length on the details of the first eight innings. You can look them up in the various record books. As is well known throughout baseball circles, the Dodgers went into the top of the ninth with a 4–3 lead and with the Yankees unable to figure out how to deal with Hugh Casey's curves. When the first two batters could not even get the ball out of the infield and Tommy Henrich now had two strikes against him, it was a leadpipe cinch that the Brooklyns would now tie the Series at two apiece.

Throughout these events we were able to keep track of the ongoing developments, due largely to a Philco radio which my new acquaintances had connected with a long extension cord running down the fire escape and into their flat below. I therefore heard Red Barber speak of such things as "cat-bird seat," "rhubarbs," "pea patches," and this and that. He was now saying that "anything can happen in Ebbets Field and usually does." Just then what he said proved to be very accurate because I saw Henrich swing and miss on the 3–2 count and so it seemed that all assembled might leave. But I also saw him drop the bat and take off very rapidly toward first base. Why was he doing this, I thought?

While we tried to learn the answer from the radio, which

could not be heard because of much yelling, the crowd from the other end of the building was racing to where we were standing to get a better view. I was not prepared for what now happened and was pushed by this surging group of individuals to the top of the aforementioned parapet. Amid much shoving, snarling, and no little amount of cursing, I found this painful and disconcerting because I looked down at the alley below with many clotheslines in between. My dime-store graph paper notebook I used to keep score flipped over the edge and I was now clutching only the eraser part of my pencil, which had been broken in two from the crush of various persons. It was all somewhat alarming.

About the time I had cause to believe that I would now soon join the notebook on the pavement below, I became aware of two things, each of which was somewhat comforting. The first of these was that the two Brooklyn fans from the fourth floor-rear had grabbed my ankles, which I doubt they would have done if they knew my true Giant identity.

The other thing I found heartening was the sound of my father yelling at the crowd. He threatened that if they did not deport themselves in a more orderly fashion it might become necessary for him to bash a skull or two. He was concerned that the falling of any citizens from this roof would create much paperwork for him besides causing him to be bawled out by his sergeant.

When things calmed down a bit, we were aware that catcher Mickey Owen had failed to hold the third strike. I learned, many years later, that the ball rolled all the way to where future SABR vice president Jack Kavanagh sat (next to Casey Stengel, but that's another story) watching. Jack was one of Larry MacPhail's ushers at the time and is still somewhat reluctant to discuss this unusual development.

But I fear I digress. What occurred next is also now history. I know only that lo these many years later it is how the observers react and the things which they say that I remember forever. Things like these:

FAT PERSON: "Owen is a bum! He should of stood in St. Louis!"

RED BARBER: "DiMaggio lines it to left…Henrich moves to…second with the tying run."

THIN PERSON: "Look at Camilli! I can tell from the way he…gestures he is yelling swear words."

ME: "Who does he swear at?"

THIN PERSON: "At the world! That is at who!"

RED BARBER: "Count 0 and 2 on Keller…There's a long drive over Walker's head against the screen in right. The Yankees go ahead 5–4."

FAT PERSON: "Why does Leo not remove Casey?"

RED BARBER: "You could boil an egg on the back of Casey's neck."

THIN PERSON: "Leo does not dare go near the mound. He fears for his life."

RED BARBER: "Ball four! Dickey draws his third walk today."

FAT PERSON: "Leo is a bum! He too should of stood in St. Louis!"

RED BARBER: "Gordon lines one over Wasdell's head in left…another double and two more runs come in."

THIN PERSON: "It is MacPhail who is a bum! Better he should of stood in Cincinnati."

RED BARBER: "Rizzuto takes ball four."

FAT PERSON: "Babe Phelps would never of left that ball get away."

THIN PERSON: "Like I say: It was MacPhail who brung all these bums here."

And on and on like that.

So, anyway, when it was all over and done with, the guys from the Bronx scored four times, the Dodgers were out 1-2-3 in the bottom of the ninth, and were now down 3–1 in the Series instead of tied. It was all very difficult to comprehend.

It was all very quiet on the roof now. As the various residents filed down the staircase to their respective flats, I heard the fat person suggest to his friend, "Leave us retire to Mulligan's saloon, where we may weep in our beers." I then heard the thin person say, "I will go by Mulligan's but I do not weep. I am a Yankee rooter!"

"Since as of when?" he inquires.

"Since as of now!" he responds.

Alas, to this very moment, I do not believe his statement to be true.

*Our eight-year-old reporter covered one of the
tightest NL pennant races of the decade*

The Gutsy
Gashouse Gang

ALDEN MEAD

It is often overlooked that the dramatic year of 1941 had a third great team, just about as good as the Yankees and Dodgers, maybe better. The St. Louis Cardinals, despite a casualty rate almost as high as the Iraqi army's, won 97 games, compared with the Dodgers' 100 and the Yanks' 101. (The fourth best was the Reds' 88.)

What's more, the Cardinals did as much as anyone to build that great Dodger team. Try to imagine the '41 Dodgers without these key players:

Pete Reiser	(.343)
Joe Medwick	(.318)
Mickey Owen	(.231)
Curt Davis	(13-7)

all of whom came from the Cardinals. (I've often thought that if the Cards had not traded away these four players, plus Johnny Mize in 1941 and Walker Cooper in 1945 and pitcher Murray Dickson in 1949, they could have won every National League pennant in the years 1941–49, except maybe 1945 when most regulars were in the service.)

Despite an incredible series of injuries, the '41 Cardinals under manager Billy Southworth fielded a fine team.

However, polls agreed in picking the Cards third, behind the Reds and Dodgers.

An early indication that the polls were wrong was the Cardinals' three-game sweep of their season opening series in Cincinnati.

The race soon resolved itself into a torrid Cardinal-Dodger affair. On June 1, after the Dodgers' Kirby Higbe outduelled the Cardinals' Max Lanier, 3–2, the teams were tied atop the standings at 31–12, .721. But the first wave of injuries had already struck the Cardinals. When the Redbirds played the Dodgers in a four-game series in St. Louis June 13–15, they had to do without catcher Walker Cooper,

home run champ Johnny Mize, and third baseman Jimmy Brown, all out with broken bones. Still, they split four games, maintaining a two-game lead.

In early July the Cards lost five straight and trailed by four games starting a two-game series in Brooklyn July 16–18 without pitcher Mort Cooper, out with elbow surgery. The Dodgers had 13-game winners Whit Wyatt and Kirby Higbe ready to administer a knockout blow.

Since the Dodgers were supposed to be weaker against lefties, Southworth started Max Lanier and rookie lefty Ernie White. The strategy apparently backfired when the Dodgers jumped to a 4-0 lead against Lanier. But the Birds got two in the fifth and routed Wyatt with five in the sixth to win.

Billy Southworth

Enos Slaughter

In game two White beat Higbe, 6-1, cutting Brooklyn's lead to two games.

Now the Dodgers faltered a bit, and when the teams next met in a two-game series in St. Louis at the end of the month, the Cards led by two. Each team won one game in addition to a 12-inning 7-7 tie.

Walker Cooper returned on July 23, and brother Mort on August 3. Mort promptly asserted himself, beating the Phils 6-1, then outduelled Bucky Walters of the Reds in 11 innings. The team was momentarily at full strength, but on August 10 right fielder Enos Slaughter collided with center fielder Terry Moore and broke his collarbone. At the end of that day's play, the Cards trailed by percentage points.

Ten days later, trailing now by two games, St. Louis played a doubleheader in Boston that proved both fateful and promising. White won the first game, 2-0, but Moore was beaned and was out for three-and-a-half weeks.

The second game saw the debut of a player who would star for the Cards for some years to come. Not Musial—he came later. Lefthanded pitcher Howard Pollet beat the Braves 3-2.

Still trailing by one-and-a-half games, and without Moore and Slaughter, the Cards managed to split a hard-fought series in Brooklyn August 24-26, with White and Cooper contributing well-pitched wins.

On August 30 at Cincinnati, Lou Warneke pitched a no-hitter allowing only one walk, and facing 28 batters (two reached on errors, but one was out stealing, the other in a double play). The last previous Redbird no-hitter had been by Paul Dean in the pennant year of 1934, so this was regarded in St. Louis as a hopeful omen. Alas, it was not to be.

With the Cards now leading by percentage points, Sportsman's Park was jammed on Labor Day by 34,812 fans, including this eight-year-old witness—the largest crowd in over two years—to see White and Pollet face the Pirates. Both survived shaky starts to win, and the Cards led by half a game.

The team could not maintain the pace, though, and had fallen three games back by September 10. Not giving up, they swept the Phils that day, while the Dodgers were getting swept in Chicago. This set up the confrontation in St. Louis Sept. 11-13, with the Cards still without Moore and Slaughter.

Mort Cooper

Johnny Mize

That famous final day

The Splendid Splinter's Splendid Finish

HARRINGTON "KIT" CRISSEY

Ted Williams

As practically all fans know, Ted Williams entered the final day of the 1941 season hitting .39955, rounded off to .400. He could have sat out a season-ending doubleheader in Philadelphia and protected his mark, but he chose to play both games, got six hits in eight at bats, and finished with a superlative .4057, rounded off to .406. Ted's magnificent day at the plate has been described again and again. Is there anything left to say?

Well, yes there is.

After going 2-for-10 at Washington and seeing his average dip to .401, Williams went 1-for-4 against the A's rookie knuckleballer Roger Wolff Saturday afternoon. This left him at .39955.

According to his autobiography, Williams took a long walk around the streets of Philadelphia that evening with Johnny Orlando, the Red Sox clubhouse boy. Manager Joe Cronin offered to take Ted out of the lineup to preserve his .400 average, but he chose to play. The next day was "cold and miserable," Williams writes, but a check of Philadelphia weather reveals just the opposite. The temperature was 82 degrees, with partly cloudy skies, 48 percent humidity. Ten thousand fans showed up that Sunday, better than the tail end A's and Phillies usually drew.

Ted needed four hits for the day to be assured of .400.

Philadelphia *Evening Bulletin* sportswriter Frank Yeutter commented before the Series that Williams faced two obstacles: (1) lengthening shadows in the autumnal afternoons and (2) unfamiliar pitchers. He later quoted Williams as saying that he had never felt nervous before but was jittery right up to the time of his first at bat on Sunday. After he got his first hit, he felt good. In his autobiography, Williams recounts how, when he stepped into the box for the first time, A's

Bill McGowan

catcher Frankie Hayes told him that Connie Mack had said if they let up on him, he'd run them out of baseball; home plate umpire Bill McGowan told him: to hit .400, a batter had to be loose.

In the opener, rookie Dick Fowler was pitching in his fourth big league game. Williams singled sharply to right his first time up and powered his 37th homer, tops in the majors, over the right field wall on his second at bat. Fowler left the game. Relieving him was twenty-two-year-old southpaw Porter Vaughan. Vaughan had pitched in 18 games for the A's the previous year with a 2–9 won-lost record, but he was appearing in only his fifth game of the 1941 season. Williams singled twice off Vaughan. At this point, he was 4-for-4!

Vaughan departed, and Tex Shirley took his place, making his fifth major league appearance. In his fifth time up, the Splendid Splinter reached first on an infield error, thus going 4-for-5 and getting on base each time.

Between games, Lefty Grove of the Red Sox was presented with a chest of silver for winning his 300th game earlier that year and also for his impending retirement.

After his hitting display in the opener, the Kid (he had turned twenty-three a month earlier) was hitting .404. While the suspense about hitting .400 was over (he could have gone 0-for-5 in the second game and still achieved his dream), Williams was ready for more action. He would be facing Fred Caligiuri, a twenty-one-year-old righthander recently brought up from the minors. Opposing him and making his last appearance in the big time would be Grove. Unfortunately, Grove didn't get past the first inning. He gave up three runs on four hits and a wild pitch before being relieved. After the A's batted in the eighth, the game was called on account of darkness (the switch from Daylight Time to Standard Time had occurred at two that morning) with the score 7–1, A's. Caligiuri had pitched a six-hitter. It was to be his second and last major league victory.

Williams went 2-for-3. He singled and hit a double off one of the loudspeaker horns at the top of the fence in right-center field. The ball broke the horn and bounded back to the field. His final average was .4057, rounded off to the .406 we remember today.

Again, it's Frank Yeutter of the Philadelphia *Evening Bulletin* reporting:

At least 2,000 persons waited around the Boston dressing room and in 21st St. to see Williams leave. He was surrounded by a mob that pinned him against the wall and made him autograph every conceivable piece of paper, book or scorecard. A couple of cops rescued him so he could make the train from North Philadelphia. But he enjoyed the ordeal and left only when he was shoved into a taxi cab.

Several Philadelphia papers, while prominently noting Ted's accomplishment in their Monday editions, gave it second billing to the Joe Louis–Lou Nova heavyweight championship fight coming up that evening. We must remember that the last man to hit .400, Bill Terry of the New York Giants, had done it just 11 years earlier.

What should we make of the mistakes in Williams's autobiography? Probably a faulty memory on Williams's part and the impossibility of having ghostwriter John Underwood check each fact of a lengthy book. But such errors tend to be

Dick Fowler

Tex Shirley

early, so Johnson took Siebert's place in the first game. Home plate umpire Bill McGowan commented after the game on how many curves I had thrown. That's true, although I don't remember exactly what pitches Williams hit. I always had a lot of confidence in my curve and wasn't afraid to throw it when behind in the count.

"In 1971, when Williams was managing the Washington Senators, a banquet was held in his honor in Washington, and a bunch of men who had played with and against him, including me, were in attendance. As soon as he saw me, he said in his characteristically loud voice, 'Where have you been for the past 30 years!' During the banquet I said I had helped make him famous that day but he hadn't returned the favor; then I laughed, handed him my realtor's card, and told him to give me a call if he was ever property hunting in the Richmond, Virginia, area."

A's pitcher Fred Caligiuri: "He was undoubtedly the best hitter I ever faced. His timing seemed to be his best asset. I was probably throwing him fastballs, as that was my best pitch. Of the two hits he got off me, the single was a humpback liner to right and the double was another line drive which hit a loudspeaker horn…. A foot or two to the left or right and it would have been a home run. Williams said afterwards it was one of the hardest balls he'd ever hit. It's well known that he was offered the chance to sit down and protect his .400 mark—one of our players, Wally Moses, sat out both games to protect a .301 average! I was twenty-one-years old at the time and was so elated about being in the majors that I wasn't too concerned about Ted Williams or the importance of the game, which has certainly grown in stature over the years."

A's outfielder Elmo Valo: "He was a marvel to watch, the best hitter I ever saw. When his drive hit the speaker in the second game, it was still in play, not a ground-rule double. The speaker was at the top of the wall and in front of it, not over it, so I think the ball would have hit the wall and bounced back or else hit the topmost part and bounced over for a homer if the loudspeaker horns hadn't been there. I don't think the ball would have cleared the wall entirely."

A's pitcher Tex Shirley: "I was called up late in the '41 season. Mr. Mack used me in relief against Washington in my first appearance in the big leagues. I just happened to get three outs on three pitches. Mack said I was his relief pitcher, and that's what I pitched for the rest of that year and the next.

"Mr. Mack asked us before the game how we wanted to play Williams, and we said we preferred to play him as a dead pull hitter; so Brancato is right when he says we had a shift on him. Bob Johnson was playing close to the first base line. Crash Davis was in the hole between first and second and the shortstop was playing on the normal side of second but close to it. If my memory is correct, the outfielders had not shifted and were playing straightaway."

repeated by subsequent writers.

To close this discourse, let's discover what those who were on the field that day have to say.

Red Sox Pitcher Broadway Charlie Wagner (Williams's roomate): "Joe Cronin wanted him to play but let him make his own decision. In our hotel room he was quiet, quieter than usual, not nervous, just very concentrated. He wondered who was going to pitch for the A's. The day turned out to be good for hitters, insofar as it wasn't bright and they didn't have to squint in the sunlight.

"Everyone on the Red Sox bench was tense and expectant every time he came up, then joyful after each hit."

A's infielder Al Brancato: "Before the first game, Mr. Mack told us not to let up on him, not to walk him. Bob Johnson, normally an outfielder, was playing first base. One of Williams's hits was a bullet hit his way. He went for the ball but couldn't quite get it. If I recall correctly, we were playing Ted well around toward right field."

A's pitcher Porter Vaughan: "Williams's first hit off me bounced over my head slightly to the right of second base and went through; the second was a hard liner to Bob Johnson's left. Johnson had been hugging the first base line but was off the bag and couldn't reach the ball. Dick Siebert, our regular first baseman, had been allowed to go home

Explosion South of the Border

Mexico's Year of Josh Gibson

GERALD F. VAUGHN

One of the most memorable in Mexican League history, 1941, was the year of Josh Gibson.. Largely on the strength of that single season, Josh was elected to the Mexican Baseball Hall of Fame in 1971—a year before his induction to the Hall of Fame at Cooperstown.

The Mexican League at that time was an independent league, which had been formed in 1925. It had advanced from amateur to semipro status, playing about a twenty-five-game schedule in the summer of 1937, forty in 1938, fifty-five in 1939. Then industrialist Jorge Pasquel entered the scene. Pasquel loved the game of baseball and envisioned a fully professional Mexican League.

In 1940 he founded the Azules team of Veracruz, managed it himself, and produced the league champion in an expanded season of ninety games. More importantly, he took control of the Mexican League. When warring factions threatened to split the league, Jorge used his considerable wealth and political influence (he was married to the daughter of a former President of Mexico) to give the league a strong sense of direction. In a bold stroke he also acquired Delta Park in Mexico City, the best baseball stadium in Mexico, exerting great leverage over other club owners by his control of access to Delta Park.

The Mexican League had been attracting increasing numbers of U.S. Negro leaguers and a few white minor leaguers to come and play for good money. In 1940 Pasquel succeeded in luring Josh Gibson to play for Veracruz in 22 games, during which Josh batted .467 with 11 home runs and 38 runs batted in.

Josh came back in 1941 and put on a batting display unequalled in Mexican League annals. Playing in 94 games (he caught and also played first base and outfield), Josh hit 33 home runs with 124 RBIs while batting .374. His home run

and runs batted in totals were not exceeded until the 145-game season of 1960.

With Gibson leading the way, the Veracruz team, managed by Lazaro Salazar in 1941, again won the pennant with a 67–35 won-lost record, finishing thirteen-and-a-half games ahead of second-place Mexico City. In the fifteen seasons of fully professional baseball (1940–1954) before the Mexican League joined U.S. organized baseball in 1955, no other pennant winner so dominated a season's play. That 1941 Veracruz team, according to the Mexican Baseball Hall of Fame, has been deemed by the majority of experts as the most powerful team to have competed in the circuit.

In addition to Josh Gibson, Veracruz had Ray Dandridge batting .367, Agustin Bejerano .366, Willie Wells .347, Lazaro Salazar .336, and Barney Brown .323. Veracruz's pitching staff was led by Barney Brown (16–5), Ramon Bragana (13–8), John Taylor (13–10), Roberto Cabal (9–1), Lazaro Salazar (7–3), and Agustin Bejerano (7–5). Brown tied with Nate Moreland of Tampico and Theolic Smith of Mexico City as the league's winningest pitcher.

Many U.S. Negro Leaguers were among the Mexican League's top players in 1941, including the great Burnis Wright. "Wild Bill" led the league's batters with .390, 17 home runs, and 85 runs batted in, playing in 100 games. He also led all outfielders in fielding percentage. Moreover he led the league's base stealers with 20.

Burnis Wright played center field for Mexico City, a team that also featured Silvio Garcia at second base. Silvio hit .366 and led the league in hits with 159. Bill Perkins (also called Cy after league catcher Cy Perkins) was the receiver and hit .308 in 97 games with 81 runs batted in. Mexico City's fine pitchers included Theolic Smith (16–8), Leroy Matlock (15–9), and Andrew "Pullman" Porter (11–16). Despite his losing

record, Porter led the Mexican League in innings pitched with 235 and strikeouts with 133. Matlock led the league with four shutouts.

Other notables around the league included Alejandro Crespo of Torreon, who led all hitters in doubles with 35. James "Cool Papa" Bell, also of Torreon, led in triples with 15, equalling the league record he set the year before.

With his 9–1 won-lost record, Roberto Cabal of Veracruz led the league's pitchers in winning percentage. Jesus Valenzuela of Tampico led in earned run average with 3.12.

At Torreon the fine Negro leagues manager and catcher Leon Ruffin led the league in fielding percentage. Unfortunately he didn't manage there, while Torreon had three managers in 1941. The first was outfielder Mel Almada, who had a lot of ability and in 1933 had been the first Mexican to play in the U.S. major leagues. Mel briefly was player-manager at Torreon, hitting .343 in 26 games before retiring from the game in mid-May. After some years away from baseball, Melo again managed in Mexico and was elected to the Mexican Baseball Hall of Fame in 1971.

Veracruz, Mexico City, Tampico, and Torreon, with most of the league's best players, finished one-two-three-four. Aguila was fifth and Monterrey sixth in the six-club league.

Josh Gibbon didn't return to play for Veracruz or any other team in the Mexican League after 1941, and Veracruz sank to last place in 1942.

Josh played his final game for Veracruz on August 31, 1941. The accompanying box score shows he played first base and caught. He went 2-for-3, including a double, with one run batted in. He also combined to take part in three double plays.

The fabled slugger had been paid $6,000 a season at Veracruz, which, according to the *Pittsburgh Courier*, was $2,000 more than he had been paid by the Homestead Grays of the Negro National League to whom he was under contract. Cum Posey and Sonnyman Jackson, officials of the Grays, had tolerated his contract jumping in the past but no more. They won a $10,000 court judgment against Josh and laid claim to his home in Pittsburgh. When Josh signed with the Grays for 1942, all was forgiven and the suit was dropped.

In 1942 Josh began to suffer from recurring headaches and blackouts. On January 1, 1943, he lapsed into a day-long coma and was hospitalized for about ten days. A brain tumor was diagnosed. Josh would not permit surgery. He resumed playing baseball and could still hit, but the headaches, blackouts, and knee problems were steadily diminishing his once unrivalled skills.

Josh Gibson died in 1947. Though he had continued to play through the 1946 season, 1941 probably was the last summer he was completely healthy. Mexico's year of Josh Gibson found him, at twenty-nine years old, at or near the peak of his legendary career.

ULTIMA ACTUACION DE GIBSON EN LA LIGA MEXICANA

Domingo 31 de agosto de 1941 segunda juego de un double-header entre Aguila y Veracruz, en el Parque Delta

BOX SCORE AGUILA VERACRUZ

	V.	C.	H.	O.	A.	E.
F. Correa, 2b	4	3	2	2	4	0
Bejerano, cf	5	1	2	3	0	0
Cardenas, ss	5	0	2	4	4	1
Molinero, 3b	5	1	4	0	1	0
Stone, cf	3	2	2	1	1	0
Wells, ss	3	1	1	6	7	0
Cocaina, rf, p	4	0	1	1	0	0
GIBSON, 1b, c	3	0	2	6	0	0
Hunter, 1b	2	1	0	5	1	0
Dandridge, 2b	4	0	0	2	5	0
S. Correa, c	2	1	1	3	3	0
Brown, rf	4	0	1	2	0	0
Aldama, 1f	2	0	0	2	0	0
Vazquez, 1f	3	0	1	0	0	0
Chicalon, 3b	3	1	1	1	3	0
Salazar, 1b	1	1	1	2	1	0
Tiant, p	2	1	1	0	3	0
Montalvo, p	2	1	0	0	1	0
Guerrero, rf	0	0	0	0	0	0
Taylor, p	1	1	1	0	0	0
Totales	**28**	**9**	**11**	**21**	**19**	**1**
Totales	**33**	**8**	**15**	**21**	**15**	**1**

Anotacion por entradas:
AGUILA   100 026 0 - 9
VERACRUZ   104 100 2 - 8

SUMARIO: Carreras producidas: Stone, Cocaina, Hunter, S. Correa, Arjona 2, Tiant 2; Bejerano, Molinero 4, Wells, GIBSON.—Bases robadas: Bejerano.—Hits de dos bases: Chicalon, Stone; GIBSON.—Hits de tres bases: Molinero, Taylor.—Double plays: Dandridge a Wells a GIBSON 2, Dandridge a Wells a Salazar, Montalvo a Wells a GIBSON.—Hits a los pitchers: a Montalvo 7 en 19 veces, a Taylor 4 en 9; a Tiant 10 en 22, a Cocaina 5 en 11.—Innings pitcheados: Montalvo 5, Taylor 2; Tiant 5, Cocaina 2.—Carreras limpias: a Montalvo 3, a Taylor 6: a Tiant 5, a Cocaina 2.—Estraqueados: Cocaina 2.—Bases por bolas: Montalvo 6, Taylor 5; Tiant 5.—Pitcher vencedor: Tiant.—Vencido: Taylor.—Umpires: Atan y Montes de Oca—Duracion: [?]—Apote: Ortigesa Jr.

Fanatico heaven

The Golden Age of Puerto Rican Ball

LUIS ALVELO

The year 1940–41, the third year of the Puerto Rican professional league, was one of the most important in our sporting history.

In our first year, 1938–39, Perucho Cepeda, Orlando's father, was crowned batting champ with a .465 average.

The decade of the 1940s saw us treated to visits by the greatest stars of Negro baseball in the United States. Our parks were filled with music and unforgettable moments.

The 1939–40 season brought Satchel Paige, who won 19 games, still a record, and Josh Gibson, who batted .380, second to Perucho Cepeda's .386. (Orlando's top mark in the same league was .362 in 1958–59.)

1940–41

More Negro league stars visited us—Monte Irvin, Roy Campanella, Billy Byrd, Buck Leonard, Bill Wright, Raymond Brown, Jud Wilson, James Green, Quincy Trouppe, Willie Wells, and others.

Puerto Rican stars included Francisco Coimbre, Luis Olmo, and Perucho Cepeda. Some of our top-caliber pitchers were Hiram Bithorn, Juan Guilbe, and Tomas Quinones.

Roy Partlow (who later pitched in the Dodger organization) was crowned batting champion at .443 (54/122). Home run leaders were Buck Leonard and Roy Campanella with 8 each. Billy Byrd won 15 games, and Dave "Impo" Barnhill struck out 193.

Our *fanaticos* were plentiful all through the 1940s. We all had our idols, and there was direct communication between the public and the ballplayers. The players held clinics without pay, visited kids in the hospital, and were very much loved by all.

The honors were given throughout the season with so much pleasure that the players remained for weeks after the campaign came to an end.

Never have I seen a group of stars who gave their all in triumph or defeat, the best decade of baseball in our island.

1941–42

George Scales wrote history in our baseball beginning this year, leading the Lions of Ponce, who had a constellation of stars from the Negro leagues. Howard Easterling, Sammy

Monte Irvin

Buck Leonard, left, with Dave Barnhill

Bankhead, and Francisco Coimbre with .360, .351, and .372 respectively, gave Scales his first of four straight championships, a record which still endures.

Josh Gibson finished as batting champ with a mark of .479 (59/123). The MVP, he connected for 13 homers. Quincy Trouppe led in RBIs with 57. Barney Brown finished with the most victories, 16, and Leon Day struck out 168 opponents.

In the winter of 1941–42, the two greatest black sluggers of their day, Josh Gibson and Willard Brown, met head-to-head for the first time. (Josh played in the Negro National League in the States, while Brown, one of the first blacks in the American League, was then playing for the Monarchs in the Negro American League.)

Brown had a long career of stardom in Puerto Rico; he holds the single-season home run record, 27, two ahead of Reggie Jackson in second place. Puerto Rican fans called Brown simply *Ese hombre*—"that man."

On January 12, 1942, he was leading the league with .441; Gibson trailed in ninth place with .355.

"Heh, Trouppe," Gibson said, "I'm not going to try to hit any home runs. I'm just going to try to bat .500." A week later Josh had moved into third place with .412 to Willard's .456. By February 9 Josh had shot into first place, .460 to .402 for Brown.

"You know what he ended up batting?" Trouppe demanded. "Four seventy-nine! He was hitting screamers through the infield."

(Some other batting averages that winter: Irvin .297, Campanella .295, Ray Dandridge .288.)

Josh's record still stands, having withstood the challenges of such great latter-day hitters as Willie Mays, Roberto Clemente, Tony Oliva, and Orlando Cepeda.

And Gibson still ended with 13 homers, also tops in the league. Brown hit 4. Josh batted in 41 runs in 31 games. Naturally they named him MVP.   —L.A.

Through today, approximately 2,083 foreign players have visited us, including Wilmer Fields, Luke Easter, Artie Wilson, Willard Brown, Willie Mays, Jim Gilliam, Sad Sam Jones, Bob Thurman, Bob Boyd, Johnny Davis, and many, many more.

When Jackie Robinson donned the flannels of the Dodgers in 1947, the teams of the Negro leagues disappeared in a short time. The absence of these stars have been some cause of regret over the years, the quality of play has never been the same again on our island. Today only our memories of excellent baseball remain.

Roy Partlow

Lots of action, lots of talent

Winter in Cuba

JORGE FIGUEREDO

Professional baseball in Cuba had an eventful year in 1941. The regular winter season, which began in October 1940 and lasted until February, saw the Havana team obtain its twenty-fifth pennant since the beginning of organized play in 1878.

Under Mike Gonzalez, the first Cuban to manage in the majors—with the Cardinals in 1938—the Lions finished seven games ahead of Santa Clara and Cienfuegos and twelve over Almendares, managed by another legendary name, Dolf Luque.

Gilberto Torres, who had played briefly during the summer for the Washington Senators, won the Most Valuable Player Award by leading the Havana pitchers with a 10–3 record in a fifty-game schedule. Torres outclassed his teammate Hall of Famer Martin Dihigo, who won 8 games. However, the winningest hurler was the Venezuelan import Vidal Lopez, at 12–5, toiling for Cienfuegos.

The top hitters were Lazaro Salazar (Almendares) .316, Silvio Garcia (Santa Clara) .314, and Carlos Blanco (Havana) .303. Another big leaguer, Bobby Estalella, led the league in doubles (13), while Carlos Blanco and Silvio Garcia hit the most triples (5). The home run crown belonged to Alejandro Crespo (Cienfuegos) with 3. A total of only 16 were hit by the whole league, as all games were played in spacious La Tropical Stadium.

American players that were seen in Havana that winter included pitchers Ace Adams and Terris McDuffie; infielders Ray Dandridge and Sam Bankhead; and outfielder "Cool Papa" Bell, who compiled a .297 batting average with 11 stolen bases.

Springtime brought the Brooklyn Dodgers to Cuba to train for their 1941 season and to host several other big league teams in exhibition games. First, the Dodgers faced the New York Giants in a three-game series that the Leo Durocher–inspired men swept over the squad headed, for the final year, by Bill Terry.

Pete Reiser was the leading batsman (.545), including a home run. Cookie Lavagetto also excelled by hitting .500 and driving in 5 runs. Lew Chiozza (.500) was the best performer for the New Yorkers, while Mel Ott was limited to a single in 7 at bats.

Juan Decall

Next came the Cleveland Indians, under Roger Peckinpaugh, and again the Dodgers breezed undefeated in three confrontations, one of them by the lopsided score of 15–0, in spite of the presence of Bob Feller on the Tribe staff.

After these six impressive performances, Durocher agreed to face a team of all-Cubans in a five-game series which ended deadlocked at two wins apiece and one tie, as indicated in the final statistics shown herewith.

As an added attraction to the fans, two other big-time clubs visited Havana in March—Cincinnati and the Boston Red Sox. The Reds were victorious twice, due to strong pitching by Johnny Vander Meer and Jim Turner.

For Boston, the only regular not to make the trip was Ted Williams, who was nursing an ankle injury suffered in a previous exhibition contest in Florida.

On March 27, the Red Sox battled against an all star selection of amateur players in what turned out to be one of the most remarkable accomplishments in Cuban baseball his-

tory: the local Davids defeated the mighty Goliaths, 2–1, on a magnificent four-hit, complete-game performance by righthanded Juan Decall, who interestingly enough never became a professional athlete.

Decall baffled the Red Sox sluggers all day, even striking out the side in the second inning, with Bobby Doerr, Jim Tabor, and Johnny Peacock as his victims.

Decall was a cute little curveball artist, who could get the ball over the plate. Local fans were disappointed. They wanted to see the big leaguers.

Later in the year, the 1941–42, there were additional significant developments in the three-team Cuban circuit, this time won by Almendares, piloted by Dolf Luque, as depicted in the accompanying statistical highlights.

Outstanding pitcher Ramon Bragana was at his best this year. Not only did he surpass Martin Dihigo in the deciding game, giving Almendares the title, but during the season he hurled four consecutive whitewashes.

BROOLYN DODGERS AGAINST ALL-CUBAN TEAM - MARCH 1941

CUBANS - Manager Jose Rodriguez

Pitchers	W - L
Gilberto Torres	1 - 0
Adrian Zabala	1 - 0
Silvino Ruiz	0 - 1
Luis Tiant	0 - 1
Rodolfo Fernandez	0 - 0

	AB	H	2B	3B	HR	RBI	AVE.
Fermin Guerra (C)	10	5	0	0	0	2	.500
Heberto Blanco (SS)	18	7	1	1	0	3	.389
Huesito Vargas (CF)	24	8	1	1	0	4	.333
Cocoliso Torres (2B)	12	4	0	0	0	1	.333
Julio Rojo (C)	3	1	0	0	0	0	.333
Saguita Hernandez (RF)	23	7	1	0	0	2	.304
Carlos Colas (C)	7	2	0	1	0	1	.286
Tony Castano (LF)	22	5	1	0	0	2	.227
Carlos Blanco (1B)	20	4	0	0	0	0	.200
Sungo Carreras (3B)	18	3	0	0	1	3	.167
Napoleon Heredia (2B)	7	1	0	0	0	1	.143
Gilberto Torres (P-SS)	7	1	0	1	0	3	.143
Roberto Ortiz (PH)	1	0	0	0	0	0	.000
TOTALS:	172	48	4	4	1	22	.279

BROOKLYN - Manager Leo Durocher

Pitchers	W - L
Steve Rachunok	1 - 0
Tex Carleton	1 - 0
Hugh Casey	0 - 1
Bill Sherer	0 - 1
Curt Davis	0 - 0
Bill Swift	0 - 0
Lefty Mills	0 - 0
Max Macon	0 - 0
Ed Head	0 - 0

	AB	H	2B	3B	HR	RBI	AVE.
Paul Waner	4	2	0	0	0	0	.500
Pee Wee Reese	2	1	0	0	0	1	.500
Charlie Gilbert	13	5	2	1	0	1	.384
Pete Reiser	8	3	1	0	0	3	.375
Mickey Owen	15	5	1	0	0	6	.333
Joe Gallagher	6	2	0	0	0	1	.333
Johnny Hudson	16	5	0	0	0	2	.313
Dolf Camilli	20	5	2	0	1	1	.250
Joe Medwick	8	2	0	0	0	2	.250
George Staller	4	1	0	0	0	0	.250
	AB	H	2B	3B	HR	RBI	AVE.
Cookie Lavagetto	15	3	1	0	0	3	.200
Lew Riggs	5	1	0	0	0	0	.200
Alex Kampouris	16	3	2	0	0	0	.188
Joe Vosmik	13	2	0	0	0	1	.154
Jimmy Wasdell	9	1	0	0	0	1	.125
Herman Franks	3	0	0	0	0	0	.000
Dixie Walker	1	0	0	0	0	0	.000
Pete Coscarat	1	0	0	0	0	0	.000
TOTAL:	158	51	9	1	1	22	.322

FINAL STATISTICS FOR REGULAR CUBAN WINTER SEASON 1941-42

	W - L	PCT.	G.B.
Almendares	25 - 19	.568	-
Habana	23 - 21	.523	2
Cienfuegos	18 - 26	.409	7

INDIVIDUAL LEADERS

Batting		Pitching
Silvio Garcia (C)	.351	
Max Macon (C)	.351	
Agapito Mayor (A)		6 - 2, .750

Times At Bat		Games Pitched
Napoleon Heredia (C)	181	
Ramon Bragana (A)		21

Runs Scored		Complete Game
Silvio Garcia (C)	24	
Ramon Bragana (A)		11
Martin Dihigo (H)		11

Hits		Games Won
Silvio Garcia (C)	60	
Ramon Bragana (A)		9

Doubles		Games Lost
Alejandro Crespo (C)	12	
Steve Rachunok (C)		9

Triples		Shutouts
Roberto Estalella (H)	4	
Ramon Bragana (A)		5

Home Runs	
Silvio Garcia (C)	4

Runs Batted In	
Roberto Estalella (H)	27

Stolen Bases	
Sungo Carreras (H)	10

Ted's Titanic All-Star Homer

GLEN STOUT

Ted Williams' home run to win the 1941 All-Star game was perhaps the most famous of his career. Fifty years after he launched a Claude Passeau slider against the roof in Detroit, the most enduring image remains his joyous romp around the bases.

Joe DiMaggio entered the game with a 48-game hit streak; Ted, with a .405 average.

The home run announced that, if the first half of the season had belonged to Joe, the second half would belong to Ted and his drive to hit .400.

Claude Passeau

Two other grand performances of the game have been almost forgotten:

- Bob Feller faced the minimum nine batters in the first three innings, giving up but one hit and striking out four.
- Pittsburgh shortstop Arky Vaughan smacked two home runs, had three hits, and knocked in four runs.

As in 1940, National league manager Bill McKechnie of Cincinnati planned what the press called a pitching "blitz," using his pitchers for no more than two innings each.

Whitlow Wyatt of Brooklyn worked the first two innings, allowing only a walk to Williams.

Paul Derringer of Cincinnati pitched a perfect third. In the fourth, Washington Senator infielder Cecil Travis doubled to left. Joe DiMaggio responded to the applause of the 54,674 fans by driving a deep fly to right-center, and Travis tagged up and took third.

Up next was Williams. He smacked a line drive directly at the Pirates' Bob Elliott, a third baseman playing left field. Riding a strong wind, the ball fooled Elliott. He started in, skidded to a halt on ground still damp from rain that morning, then started to race back before slipping down. The ball sailed over his head as Williams was credited with a double, giving the American League a 1–0 lead.

Bucky Walters of the Reds pitched the fifth and sixth. He led off the top of the sixth with a double to left. The Cubs' Stan Hack sacrificed, and the Cardinals' Terry Moore brought Walters home with a long fly to Williams, who nearly threw out Walters at home.

But Bucky let the American Leaguers go ahead again in the bottom of the inning. DiMaggio walked, Williams flew out, Jeff Heath of the Indians walked, and Joe scored on a single by Lou Boudreau of Cleveland.

In the seventh, Enos Slaughter of the Cardinals drove the first pitch toward Williams, who followed Elliott's example and slipped, allowing Slaughter to take second on the error.

Pittsburgh's Arky Vaughan was next. He was hitting .300 but had only four home runs and had been only a part-time player, as manager Frankie Frisch inexplicably preferred to split the shortstop position between Vaughan and light-hitting Alf Anderson.

Vaughan stroked a pitch down the right-field line. It landed in the first row of the upper deck, fair by 15 feet, and the National League led, 3–2.

Righthander Claude Passeau of the Cubs, a pioneer of the slider, was next in McKechnie's pitching rotation, and he set the American Leaguers down in order in the seventh.

In the top of the eighth, the Cardinals' Johnny Mize doubled to right. Vaughan stepped to the plate and again drove the ball toward right, this time higher and deeper. It disappeared into the crowd halfway up the second deck, and Vaughan vaulted around the bases, giving the National League a 5–2 lead.

But the game was not over. After Travis fouled out to lead off the AL eighth, DiMaggio pleased the crowd by doubling to left-center. The crowd cheered loud and long for Joe as Williams stepped up to the plate.

Williams always said his most difficult at bats were against pitchers with whom he was unfamiliar. In a season in which he would strike out only 27 times, Ted was caught looking at a Passeau slider. Thinking the pitch was low, he protested mildly to NL umpire Babe Pinelli.

Ted's Boston teammate, Dom DiMaggio, followed Williams, the first time brothers had ever appeared in an All Star game, and singled in Joe to make it 5–3. Boudreau followed with a hit to center that Brooklyn's Pete Reiser fumbled, putting runners on second and third.

Up stepped Jimmie Foxx of Boston. Three pitches later, Foxx followed Williams' path to the dugout. The National League was three outs away from victory.

Then McKechnie blinked. He backed off from his pitching "blitz" and allowed Passeau to pitch the ninth, although he had Lon Warneke and Carl Hubbell available. Passeau's strikeouts of Williams and Foxx had impressed him.

In the ninth, the A's Frankie Hayes popped out. Cleveland's Ken Keltner slapped a hard ground ball to short. The Boston Bees' Eddie Miller, a defensive replacement for Vaughan, let the ball hit his chest, and Keltner reached first. The Yankees' Joe Gordon singled to right, and Travis walked to load the bases.

DiMaggio stepped to the plate, the stage set for him to add to an illustrious year. But he grounded sharply to short. Miller flipped to Brooklyn's Billy Herman at second to start a double-play and end the game.

However, Travis took Herman out with a hard slide, and Billy's throw was wide. DiMaggio was safe, and Keltner scored to make it 5–4.

Members of the press expected McKechnie to replace the right-handed Passeau with the lefty, Hubbell, whom Ted had never seen before. But McKechnie didn't move. Would he walk Williams, with Dom DiMaggio up next? That would have put the winning run on second. Passeau pitched to Ted.

The first pitch was low. Ted fouled off the next offering and admonished himself to be quicker. Passeau says the next pitch was a slider, letter-high and in. Ted was quick.

The ball rose high down the line, battling a cross-wind, as Williams loped toward first, his head lifted, following the flight of the ball. The ball hit the roof, 118 feet above the field, hung for a split second in the bunting, then dropped to the field, a home run. (The blow was inches from clearing the roof. If it had, it would have been only the second ball to do so. The first was struck by Williams himself in 1939. The feat would not be done again until Mickey Mantle in 1957.)

WHAT HAPPENED TO THE BALL?

Right-fielder Enos Slaughter picked up Williams' home run ball and put it on his mantelpiece in North Carolina. Forty-four years later at Slaughter's own induction to Cooperstown, in 1985, he took the ball from his pocket, turned, and presented it to Ted.

Williams half ran, half leaped around the bases, his arms forming gigantic circles. When he reached the plate, his teammates came out, clasping hands and slapping him.

In the clubhouse, AL manager Del Baker of Detroit kissed Williams. DiMaggio punched him in the arm. Joe Cronin wandered about in a daze, telling everyone that Ted was great.

Williams talked and talked—about the hit, about his mother, about the hit, about the pitch, about the hit, about his strikeout, about the hit, about his great throw, about the hit—unable to restrain his joy.

With that swing, Ted announced himself. He was no longer a young hitter of promise but a hitter who was suddenly seen as special.

DID TED CALL HIS SHOT?

Williams, who went 0-for-2 in the 1940 game, had been telling teammate Jimmie Foxx for days that he thought he was going to bust loose in the '41 contest.

Before Arky Vaughan's final at bat, Ted says, he "had a feeling" that Arky would park one.

Even after Ted's eighth-inning strikeout, losing by three runs, Williams says he still thought he'd get another chance to bat. "I had this funny feeling that I was going to get up there at least one more time and hit one. I get hunches that way. I never say anything about 'em, and as sure as I do, they don't come true." He had been right about Vaughan. "Something seemed to tell me he was gonna do that. Well, I figured I was going to get up there again."

John B. Holway
The Last .400 Hitter

Injuries kill the Cards

Showdown in St. Louis

BILL BORST

By June 1, 1941, the Cardinals clung to a one-game lead. But they should have replaced their logo with a "Blue Cross" as injuries decimated their lineup.

Catcher Walker Cooper broke his shoulder and appeared in just 67 games.

His brother, pitching stalwart Mort, had Dr. Robert Hyland, "the Surgeon General of Baseball," cut growths out of his elbow, knocking him out of action from June 17 to August 3.

Another pitcher, Howie Krist, also had his arm restored by Dr. Hyland.

First baseman Johnny Mize broke a finger and injured his shoulder; his home runs dropped from 43 to 15.

Rookie second baseman Creepy Crespi also broke a finger and suffered facial lacerations from a batted ball.

Third baseman Jimmy Brown joined the crowd and broke a bone in his right hand.

Still, by July 1 the Cards and Dodgers were deadlocked.

The blows that probably cost St. Louis the pennant were dealt to its outfield. On August 10 Enos Slaughter, who was as "hot as a barn fire," leading the club in homers and RBI's, crashed into team captain Terry Moore. Moore was only shaken up, but Slaughter broke his collarbone.

Ten days later Braves lefty Artie Johnson exploded a fastball against Moore's skull. Neither outfielder saw much action the rest of the season.

Only "Mr. Shortstop," Marty Marion, played the season's full 155 games.

Southworth, the greatest manager to come out of Harvard, Nebraska, juggled his lineup so masterfully that *The Sporting News* named him Manager of the Year. Johnny Hopp and Estel Crabtree filled in ably, but it became apparent during the final Brooklyn series that the bench could not compensate for the loss of the outfield mainstays.

The Dodger lead was never much more than a game throughout early September.

The season centered on the teams' final series in St. Louis, starting September 11. National League president Ford Frick was there to set the rules for a playoff if needed.

The local press termed it the "Little World Series," borrowing a headline from a series between the Browns and Yankees in 1922—St. Louisians remembered only too well

Howie Krist

how the Yankees had come into the city with a one-game lead and had won two out of three. Baby Doll Jacobson, star center fielder of that Browns team, visited the Cardinal locker room.

Fans brought cowbells, and one had a horn that sounded like a "Bronx cheer." The crowd lustily booed their former idol, Ducky Medwick, now wearing a Dodger uniform. A number of fights broke out.

The Cards tied the game on Dodger errors in the seventh, as Brooklyn hurler Freddy Fitzsimmons exhorted his teammates in the old Leo Durocher style. The game threatened to deteriorate into a brawl like the last series in Brooklyn, and the umpires warned both managers about excessive protests.

With Brooklyn's Hugh Casey pitching superb relief, the teams went into the 11th tied, 4–4, when Dixie Walker batted in a pair to win it, 6–4.

In game two St. Louis rookie Howie Pollett (20–3 at Houston's Texas League club) faced ex-Card Curt Davis. The crowd screamed disapproval when Southworth removed Pollett during a Brooklyn rally in the sixth. Lefty Max Lanier put out the fire, shutting the Dodgers down the rest of the way. His curve was so sharp that he had Pete Reiser diving in the dirt on a pitch that broke over the plate for a

Marty Marion

Creepie Crespi, making like Enos Slaughter

called third strike. The Dodgers avoided pitching to Mize, but the Cards rallied to defeat Davis, 4–3.

As in 1922, the series hinged on the rubber game. Both Moore and Slaughter took batting practice. "Country" lofted three over the pavilion roof, but admitted that catching a ball pained him.

Brooklyn's Whitlow Wyatt, seeking his 20th win, faced Mort Cooper before a capacity crowd of over 31,000. Cooper carried a no-hitter into the eighth inning when Dixie Walker hit a double that fell just in front of Johnny Hopp, who was playing center in place of Moore. Billy Herman followed with another two-bagger to the same spot for a 1–0 lead.

Tempers flared again when Crespi, dodging an inside pitch, popped up to Dolph Camilli at first. As he passed the Brooklyn bench, coach Charley Dressen and the Dodgers "gave him the works," and umpire Babe Pinelli had to restrain him from charging the bench.

Still losing, the Cards sent Slaughter up to pinch-hit in the ninth, but Wyatt fanned him to win the game, 1–0.

The loss dropped the Cards two games behind. St. Louis had 10 of its last 16 games at home; Brooklyn would play 12 of its remaining 14 on the road, but most of them against the hapless Phils and stingless Bees.

The Cards swept a doubleheader from Boston, 6–1 and 3–2, as Crabtree hit a homer in the ninth to win the nightcap. It was also Stan Musial's first major-league game. They were now one game behind.

St. Louis had a chance to slip into first on the 16th, but Frank Demaree of Boston hit a three-run homer to beat them, 4–1.

Next Lon Warneke went into the ninth winning 3–1 against the Cubs. Krist relieved, but Chicago's Bob Scheffing hit a grand slam to win. The loss dashed any hope of catching Brooklyn as Wyatt beat Boston, 6–0, to clinch the flag, the Dodgers' first in 21 years.

The two Negro Leagues in 1941

Before the Game Was Color Blind

TODD BOLTON

Although Josh Gibson and other stars jumped to Mexico, the Negro leagues boasted plenty of action from players who, only a few years later, would make headlines in the white major leagues.

Negro baseball consisted of twelve teams and two leagues. According to Effa Manley, co-owner of the Newark Eagles, it cost a half million dollars to operate each league. Wilson was the official ball, each team had its own bus, and two uniforms for each player was the norm. The season lasted from May to September, and each team tried to play about forty league games, plus inter-league games. The remainder of the contests each year were exhibition games, mostly against semi-pro teams.

In 1941, Satchel Paige came back from a three-year sore arm that had almost ended his career and posted an 8–1 mark to lead the Kansas City Monarchs to their third straight pennant in the Negro American (Western) League.

In the East, Monte Irvin of the Newark Eagles hit .380 to take the batting championship in the Negro National League. * All stats have been reconstructed from box scores but were not known to the fans at the time.)

And twenty-old Roy Campanella, already in his fourth season with the Baltimore Elite Giants, won the MVP award in the East-West, or All Star, Game before 50,000 fans at Comiskey Park.

The Monarchs and the Gibson-less Washington Homestead Grays again dominated the two leagues.

Satchel showed the speed and control that made him a legend. During 67 innings pitched, Old Satch struck out 61, highest in the league, and walked only six.

Paige was also collecting his biggest paychecks. The Baltimore *Afro-American* stated that Paige was probably the highest paid player in all of baseball, earning over $37,000 a year. (Hank Greenberg, white baseball's highest paid player in 1940 at $40,000, was in the Army. Joe DiMaggio replaced Hank as tops in '41 with $35,000.) Paige started 11 games that year but completed only three. The Monarchs had already begun to capitalize on his drawing power by advertising him to start, then bringing in a reliever. It probably hurt Satchel's victory total, since he often didn't pitch the minimum innings needed for a victory.

Satchel Paige

But Paige wasn't the best black pitcher in baseball, nor even on the Monarchs. Hilton Smith, Paige's relief man, went 10–0 to lead the league in percentage for the third time in five years. He also saved three games. (Monarch rookie Connie Johnson, who later pitched for the White Sox and Orioles, was 2–2.)

The Birmingham Black Barons' Dan Bankhead, in his second year in the league, had a 6–1 record. Six years later he would become the first black pitcher in the white major leagues, with Brooklyn.

Barons outfielder Lyman Bostock, also in his second year, ran away with the Western batting title, hitting .375. His son would later play for Minnesota and California.

Other leading hitters included Kansas City's Ted Strong, a Harlem Globetrotter in the off-season, at .357, and the Monarchs' Willard Brown, who batted .333 and was tops in home runs in the West. In 1947 Brown, then thirty-six, became one of the first blacks in the American League, playing briefly with the St. Louis Browns.

In the East, the Grays' defending batting champ, Buck Leonard, fell off to .234, although he led in home runs. Their great pitcher, Raymond Brown, 13–6, carried the team to victory in the first half of the split season.

The Newark Eagles lost veterans Ray Dandridge and Willie Wells to Mexico but still finished second.

A twenty-two-year old out of Lincoln University, Monte Irvin, had come up with the Eagles in 1939 and hit .403. In '41 he took the batting title with .380.

Veteran pitcher Leon Day, back after a 12–1 season in Venezuela, pitched and played outfield. He was 1–1 on the mound and hit .336.

Campanella batted a sturdy .368 for the third-place Baltimore Elite Giants.

As usual, the highlight of the season was the annual East-West all star game. Newspapers reported that this was "the hottest voting campaign" in the nine-year history of the event. Paige led the vote-getters for the West, and little Dave "Impo" Barnhill, 9–6 with the New York Cubans, was tops in the East. Each received over 95,000 votes.

Paige and Barnhill had once barnstormed together against the American Association Toledo Mudhens. When

Satchel blanked the Hens for five innings, the Toledo manager asked his counterpart to "put in the little guy," and Barnhill blanked them the last four innings. The Toledo skipper was upset. "You just took Satchel out behind the stands and cut off his legs," he said.

The East-West game was played in Comiskey Park in 97-degree heat, but even with the sweltering conditions, it attracted 50,000, the largest crowd ever to see a black sporting event. An additional 5,000 fans were turned away.

The East won the game, 5–3, led by Barnhill's pitching, Campanella's defensive play, and Leonard's home run. Paige pitched just two innings for the West, and he gave up one hit, to Campanella.

The Cubans edged the Eagles for the second-half title and played the Grays at Yankee Stadium for the league pennant. Brown won, 2–0, for the Grays' fifth straight flag.

Unfortunately, no World Series was played.

It would be six years before baseball's barriers would crumble and some of the heroes of '41 would eventually have their opportunities to play in the majors. For others—Day, Leonard, Hilton Smith—it would be too late.

H.G. Salsinger, sports editor of the Detroit News, after viewing a doubleheader between the Elites and Grays, wrote:

"Colored cultural organizations have been trying to beat down the color line and gain admittance for colored ball players to major league rosters. The answer to all their campaigns has been that the colored league lacked players capable of making the big-league grade.

"Here was a chance to compare the play of the colored leaguers with that of the major leaguers, and the comparison, made after more than five hours of competition, was in favor of the colored players.

"There is one thing that distinguishes the Negro National League ball players from their major league brethren, and that is their whole-hearted enthusiasm and their genuine zest. They play baseball with a verve and flair lacking in the big leagues. They look like men who are getting a great deal of fun out of it but who desperately want to win."

Had America been color blind in 1941, we can only imagine what a season it could have been.

Or maybe it was Steve

Stan the Boy

RALPH HORTON

When the Cardinals' newest rookie, Stan Musial, reported on September 16, he had a hard time convincing Terry Moore and Johnny Mize that he was the wild young lefthander off whom they had hit long home runs in an exhibition game in early April.

The twenty-year old Musial had been an 18-game winner as a pitcher with Daytona Beach in 1940, had played the outfield when he wasn't pitching, and had batted .311. Late in the season, however, he injured his left shoulder making a diving catch. He went to spring training fearful that his career might be over.

After giving up the homers to Moore and Mize, Musial never pitched again (until the last game of 1952).

There was not much demand for a sore-armed hurler, but Springfield in the Western Association had a spot in the outfield, and Stan hit .379 there. Moving up to Rochester, he continued to hit at a .326 clip.

Cardinal manager Billy Southworth was in desperate need of outfield help, with Moore and Enos Slaughter both injured, and called Stan to St. Louis.

On the morning of September 17 the Cardinals were only a game and a half behind Brooklyn with thirteen to play. It was a warm day, with temperatures in the 70s, but despite the close pennant race, only 3,505 turned out for the double-header against the seventh-place Boston Braves.

The Cardinals won the first game, but the Dodgers also won, so St. Louis had to win the second game to gain ground.

The Associated Press reported that "Steve Musial" was playing right field in the nightcap. Southworth placed him third in the batting order between Johnny Hopp and Mize against Jim Tobin (12–12).

In the first inning Tobin threw the kid his best pitch: a knuckler. "I didn't know what it was," Stan recalled. "I had never seen one before. The best I could do was pop one up to the third baseman."

In the third inning the score was 0–0 and two men were on. This time, "I knew what was coming and lined the knuckler off the left-field screen," driving in both runners.

Stan also had a single to go 2-for-4, and the Cardinals won the game, 4–2, on Estel Crabtree's ninth-inning home run, putting them only a game out of the lead.

Stan went on to make 3,628 more hits and 724 more doubles—a National League record—while leading the Cards to four pennants and three world championships.

His .426 average for twelve games in '41 was the highest in either league and topped Ted Williams by 20 points.

Baseball's saddest story

The Funeral of Lou Gehrig

GARRETT J. KELLEHER

Everything seemed so fitting.

It rained.

The Yankees did not play; they were in Detroit, where Lou Gehrig's consecutive game playing streak had ended two years earlier.

The funeral service was private and modest. Not more than one hundred relatives, friends and baseball people attended the Episcopal service in Christ Church in the Riverdale section of the Bronx. There was no eulogy, at the request of the family. The Rev. Gerald V. Barry did pause to say, "We need none, because you all knew him." The ceremony lasted less than ten minutes. The coffin was then taken to the Fresh Pond Crematory in Middle Village, in Queens. Interment was at Kensico Cemetery in Valhalla, New York.

Lou's father and mother were the first family members to arrive. Preceding Eleanor, Lou's widow, were the honorary pallbearers, including Bill Dickey; Joe McCarthy; Andy Coakley, Lou's baseball coach at Columbia; John Kieran of *The New York Times*; Bill Robinson, the famous tap dancer; and a Deputy Mayor of New York.

The small assemblage also included league presidents Will Harridge and Ford Frick; Ed Barrow, George Ruppert and George Weiss, of the Yankees; Bill Terry of the Giants; and Eddie Collins. The youngest person was Timothy Sullivan, the Yankee batboy.

Lou died at his home, 5204 Delafield Avenue in beautiful, affluent Riverdale, on Monday, June 2nd at 10:00 PM. He would have celebrated his thirty-eighth birthday on June 19. All the entrances of the home could have been fitted with ramps and the stairways adapted to a wheelchair. However, Lou could not think of living this way, and a wheelchair was never brought to the house.

This house was a scene of entertainment nearly every night for the last two years of Lou's life. An open bar and buffet was set up and show business people came and did their routines for the Gehrigs in order to keep things light and lively. However, sobriety was adhered to and lights went out at eleven. Two of the most frequent visitors were Kieran and actress Tallulah Bankhead.

The day after Lou died, his body was viewed for three hours at the Church of the Divine Paternity, Central Park West and 76th Street. The original plans had been that there would be no public viewing. However, when it became obvious that there was great public sentiment, the ban was lifted. The body was then moved to Christ Church. A line of three blocks formed outside the church and from 8:00 to 10:00 PM, an estimated 5,000 people filed past the casket.

The year of 1941, which was witness to so many great baseball events, was also witness to one of the saddest and most untimely deaths in the history of the game.

Intimations of things to come

The Midnight Sun

OSCAR EDDLETON

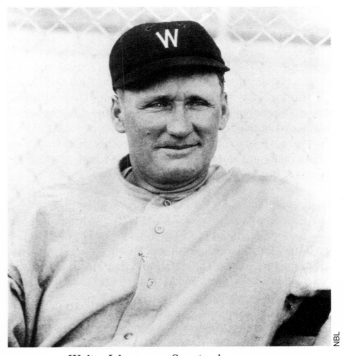

Walter Johnson, as Senators' manager

On May 28 Washington Senators owner Clark Griffith watched Walter Johnson throw a fastball, breaking an electron beam, which turned on "the midnight sun" to the ooh's and ah's of a capacity crowd of 25,000 at the Senators' Griffith Stadium.

It was the first night game in the history of Washington, the eleventh major league team to install electric lights. (Joe DiMaggio got one hit, a triple, to run his streak to 13 games.)

Thirty-two years earlier, in 1909, Griffith, then manager of the Cincinnati Reds, had watched a primitive night game in the Reds' park. It "will never rival the daylight article," Griff had sniffed.

On July 17, 1941 in Cleveland, another nighttime throng of 67,468 in Municipal Stadium witnessed the end of DiMaggio's streak. It was the largest crowd for a night game up to that time.

Each team was allowed only seven night games a year. In 1941, 1.5 million fans witnessed the seventy-seven night games in the National League (six clubs) and American League (five clubs). The average per game was over 20,000. These were impressive figures indeed.

By year's end Griffith was begging for permission to play more games under the lights.

Clark Griffith: the Old Fox changed his tune.

Brothers in the outfield

¡Caramba! Here Come Los Hermanos Alous

BOB RUCK

The 1966 season was a good one for Dominicans, and no family from Hispaniola had a better one than the Alous.

Brothers Mateo and Felipe finished one-two in the National League batting race, the first time that has ever happened in major league history. Mateo won it, the first Dominican ever to do that. Their compatriot, Rico Carty, finished third and Puerto Rican Roberto Clemente tied for fourth in this unprecedented Latin sweep:

Mateo Alou	PIT	.342
Felipe Alou	ATL	.327
Rico Carty	ATL	.326
Roberto Clemente	PIT	.317

Jesus Alou, the younger sibling, finished back in the back at .259 but he played leftfield for the San Francisco Giants, who fought the Dodgers and Mateo's Pirates for the National League pennant.

In addition, Dominican Juan Marichal, 25–6 with the Giants, was tops in the league in winning percentage at .806. Without the Latins in the league, Los Angeles would have won the pennant easily. As it was, they just beat the Giants by 1.5 games and the Pirates by three.

All in all, Latin fans found that comfortably perusing box scores with a cafe con leche under the tropical sun had never been so good.

The Alous could always hit. In their combined 46 major league seasons, they were good for 5,094 hits, 1,656 RBI's and 2,213 runs scored. In Dominican winter play, they logged another 47 campaigns. During that span, they won four batting crowns, and at one time or another led the league in home runs, RBIs, doubles, triples, total bases, slugging, and stolen bases.

Aficionados consider Felipe's 1958–59 season, when he led the league in hitting, doubles, triples, total bases, slugging, and stolen bases, the finest Dominican winter season ever put together.

As proud as their compatriots were of the Alous' winter play, they were enthralled by their remarkable 1966 major league performances.

It is often said in the Dominican Republic that there will never be political disturbances during baseball season, only afterwards. But in 1965 there had been no winter season at all as first a civil war and then the U.S. Marines' invasion stopped business as usual. The catalyst of this revolution was the struggle to bring back the legally elected government of Juan Bosch, who had been deposed in a 1963 coup.

But 1966 found peace restored, albeit with a dose of repression, and a full complement of islanders was playing in the majors. With the 1965–66 winter season abandoned, the '66 major league season took on added significance.

The Alous were from Haina, a port west of Santo Domingo dominated by a huge sugar mill refinery. But the Alous escaped the canefields by way of the ballfields, joining the growing ranks of Dominican ballplayers heading for North American ballfields.

Felipe, 31 in 1966, was the first Alou to go, arriving in the minors in 1956 and debuting with the Giants two years later. The 6'1", 195-pound outfielder combined fine defensive play with speed and power.

Mateo, 27, three inches shorter and 35 pounds lighter, was more of a contact hitter. He had joined Felipe on the Giants in 1960.

Jesus, 24, the tallest of the three, had become the third Alou on the Giants in 1963. On September 10, in a game against the Mets, the Alous became the first three brothers to play for the same major league team at the same time.

Jesus Alou, left, joins his brothers, Mateo and Felipe in the Giants' outfield, September, 1963.

Their lifetime records:

	Yr	G	HR	BA
Felipe	17	2082	206	.286
Mateo	15	1667	31	.307
Jesus	15	1380	32	.280

Jesus, whose major-league stats fall below his brothers', surpassed them in winter play. He has more hits than any Dominican winter leaguer and is third in RBI's and is one of only four men to play for 20 winter seasons.

The 1966 NL campaign was their finest season:

	Team	G	R	H	2B	3B	HR	RBI	SB	BA	Rank@
Mateo	Pit	141	86	183	18	9	2	27	23	.342*	3
Felipe	Atl	154	122*	218*	31	6	31	74	5	.327	5
Jesus	SF	110	41	96	13	1	1	20	5	.259	1

@ Team rank

Mateo played center field between Clemente and Willie Stargell. The diminutive Dominican's job was to get on base. His power stats pale before those of Felipe, but the Pirates stayed in the tight three-way race for the pennant.

Felipe also led the league in total bases. He split his time between the outfield and first base.

Jesus played left field beside Willie Mays.

That winter Mateo returned to the Dominican Republic and added the winter batting crown. In so doing, he broke Manuel Mota's three consecutive championships.

Mateo and Felipe almost duplicated their feat in 1968, but Pete Rose edged Mateo out for the crown, .335 to .332. Felipe finished third at .317.

The '60s were a remarkable decade for Latin hitters. They won eight batting titles, with Clemente alone copping four. Virtually every year a Latin was in the top three in the batting races. Clemente (NL) and Cuban Tony Oliva (AL) won consecutive crowns in 1964 and '65.

THE ALOUS VS. THE WANERS

Only the Waner brothers have collected more major league hits than the Alous:

	G	H		G	H
Paul Waner	2549	3152	Felipe Alou	2082	2101
Lloyd Waner	1993	2459	Mateo Alou	1667	1777
Jesus Alou	1380	1216			
	4542	5611		5109	5094

BROTHERS AND SONS

Dominicans have sent a number of brother acts to U.S. pro ball, including Diomedes and Chi Chi Olivo, Pascual and Melido Perez, George and Juan Bell, Tony and Ramon Pena, and Teddy and Ramon Martinez (still in the minors).

Felipe Alou's son, Moises, of the Expos, represents the second generation of Dominican ballplayers who are sons of major leaguers. Others are Stan Javier, Pedro Borbon, Jr., and the several sons of Manual Mota: Jose, Andy, Domingo, and Gary Mota are already playing pro ball, and Rafael 16, and Antonio, 13, might join them some day. Perhaps they will surpass the Alou brothers as the greatest Dominican brother act in baseball.

A Year to Forget For Yankee Fans

© 1991

VIC DEBS

After watching their team win the pennant for five straight seasons, 1960 to 1964, Yankee fans were stunned by the club's sixth-place finish in 1965. Little did we know that the "Bombers" would leave us in an even bigger state of shock the following year—finishing with a 70–89 record, one of the worst in the history of the organization. It left them in last place for the first time in over fifty years and left fans searching for the causes and the scapegoats.

Manager Johnny Keane was the logical culprit to point fingers at. He wasn't liked much by fans in the first place. In 1964, his Cardinal team had the audacity to upset the favored pinstripers in an exciting seven-game World Series. When he switched ships to the Yanks the following year, and the Yanks failed to make it into the Fall Classic for only the second time in eleven years, New Yorkers were even less keen on Keane. But when their superstar hero Mickey Mantle showed no enthusiasm either, and the team got off to a horrid beginning in 1966, the handwriting was on the wall. Soon the predictable occurred, and likable Ralph Houk resumed the helm in early May.

When the Yanks responded by winning their next three games, it looked as though the Major had been the perfect stimulus for the apathetic athletes. Unfortunately, the team soon reverted to their losing ways, doing little better under Houk (66–73 compared to 4–16 under Keane). Additionally, since the Bombers' record was nearly identical in 1967 (72–90), it doesn't seem accurate to lay blame on Keane for the embarrassment of '66. Better to look for other reasons. If not the managers, it's the play of the players, notably the stars, who must be scrutinized.

Mantle had been the best player on the Yankees for sixteen seasons, and many would argue, the premiere in the game for most of those years. He led them to a dozen pennants and seven World Championships. But his numbers for that notorious 1966 season would appear to be incriminating evidence. The Oklahoman managed only 23 round-trippers that year, batted .288, around 20 points below his career average at that time, and knocked in a mere 56 runs, his third lowest total up to that point. Yet, injuries forced the Mick to miss more than 50 games. Projecting his stats over the course of 162 games, Mantle had an excellent year. He would have finished with 34 homers, 84 RBIs, close to 90 walks, 270 total bases, and 140 hits. Keeping in mind that opposing pitchers were avoiding throwing strikes to him, preferring to face other swingers in that anemic lineup, his production looks even more impressive.

Just as telling was how the team performed during the first half of the season, when the then-healthy Mick was doing most of his damage with the lumber. By the All-Star break, he had 18 four-baggers. Included was a one-week stretch when Mantle went on a home run surge which Mark Gallagher in his book *Explosion* describes as "the best power spree since Roger Maris hit seven homers in six games in 1961. Mantle was hitting homers at the greatest rate in American League history." Despite his first-half heroics, however, the team was floundering in seventh place by mid-July, nineteen games behind first place and only four games from the bottom.

The biggest trouble spots were age and injuries. Besides thirty-four-year-old Mantle, Bobby Richardson, Elston Howard, and Roger Maris were all over thirty. Richardson's subpar performance may have been caused in part by a lack of motivation. It was common knowledge that he preferred retirement to continued service with the Yanks when the '66 season opened.

Although a bad knee forced Maris to miss half the sea-

son, abusive treatment by the fans may have ruined his concentration while he was able to play. Due in part to insinuations by the Yankee organization, the fans believed Roger wasn't really hurting, but instead was using the injury as an excuse to dog it on the field. Subsequently, he was often the target of their boos and "Bronx" cheers. After he homered to help win a game in mid-August, some of the fans let him hear it while he circled the bases, prompting an angry Maris to respond afterward, "They've been giving it to me ever since I came here. I've given everything I have every time I take the field. I made them unhappy when I hit 61 home runs, now I guess I made them unhappy by hitting this homer. I couldn't care less."

At age thirty-seven, Elston Howard was showing his age. Often overlooked and underrated by fans, Ellie's efforts during the '64 season led to the Yankees' successful pennant bid more than anyone else's. It was his inability to produce that may have had the most dramatic effect on the team in '66. A comparison of his stats in 1964 and 1966 verifies this:

	HR	RBI	BA
1964	15	84	.313
1966	6	35	.256

It saddened me when they traded him to Boston. He left soon after Mantle hit his 500th home run, the most thrilling moment in sports for me. Ellie was the first player to congratulate the Mick after crossing home plate. I'm glad he was. Howard was a ballplayer with class.

Just as significant was the inability of the youth to pick up the slack. Instead of blossoming into stardom, as had been the tradition on Yankee teams of the past, the young players were failing. At first base, Joe Pepitone was the exception. The twenty-five-year-old had a career-high of 31 homers in '66, accompanied by 83 RBIs and a steady glove.

Tom Tresh, twenty-eight, was a disappointment. Tommy's impressive home run total of 27 is deceiving; his low batting average (.233) was more indicative of his lack of production, and he was unable to deliver clutch hits in numerous situations.

Roy White played his first full season in 1966 but it's one he's probably willing to forget, since he hit a mere .225 with 20 RBIs.

The Yankee pitchers fared no better. Whitey Ford, Mel Stottlemyre, Al Downing, and Jim Bouton had all been part of the pennant celebration of 1964 but suffered through the agony of '66 as well.

Stottlemyre's inability to win is particularly difficult to understand. The year before he was a 20-game winner and Cy Young candidate. He would have two more 20-game seasons in 1968 and 1969. His lifetime ERA was an outstanding 2.97. A case could be made for Stot being the best Yankee pitcher ever. But what happened in 1966?

Early-season frustration may have been the reason. Al-though Mel began the year winning five of his first eight decisions, he pitched well enough to have won even more. His first loss was a 3–1 decision, followed by a 2–1 defeat. His only loss in May was by a 4–2 score. In two no-decision games, the Yanks lost, 3–2 and 2–1. With any luck he could have been 8-1 or 7-2 by the end of May. He continued pitching well in June, but his record suffered nonetheless. On June 5, he pitched six innings, giving up two earned runs but he was not involved in the decision. In his next appearance, he lost a 2–1 heartbreaker, and after winning 5–2, he was again a victim of a 2–1 setback, giving up only four hits in nine innings.

"I'm not alibiing," Mel said, "but things have happened to me this year that never happened to me before. Balls bouncing through the infield or blooping in, usually at a time when it hurts." Just as a pitcher has to have some luck in order to win 20, he has to have some bad luck to lose 20.

What happened to Stottlemyre seemed to happen to everyone on the team that year. Everything just kept on going wrong. One play exemplified how snakebitten the pinstripers were. It occurred in late June in the first game of a doubleheader at the Stadium. The Yanks were trailing 7–5 going into the final frame. They managed to get two men on, and with two outs, White came to bat representing the winning run. Batting lefthanded, he pulled a drive heading toward the stands. The right fielder leaped for the ball, disappearing in the seats. Roy began his home run trot while Houk charged out of the dugout with right hand extended ready to congratulate him. Suddenly the right fielder came out of the stands holding the ball in the air. Umpire Hank Soar stopped rotating his index finger signalling a homer and showed a clenched fist instead, signifying an out. Houk changed the direction of his charge, now heading toward Soar at full steam. The call stood, and the Yanks lost yet another ballgame. Their opponents that day were the soon-to-be world champion Baltimore Orioles, and the right fielder who stole the game from them was the Triple Crown and MVP winner of 1966, Frank Robinson.

Clete Boyer, in an Old Timers' Day interview in 1990, was asked to comment on the Yankees' last-place finish in 1966. Said Cletis, "It was frustrating as hell. It was almost unbelievable." That's the way everyone felt—players, writers, fans, and even Yankee-haters. No one could believe or even accept it. Yet many teams had occupied the cellar in the past without being subjected to as much scoffing and criticism. Why were the Yanks targeted? After all, it was something they hadn't done for fifty-four years. How many other franchises could make that boast?

I guess it's the price you pay for being the best, that everyone expects you to stay the best or at least never become the worst. Still, the Bombers were my favorite team when spring training opened in 1967. They remain my favorite in spite of their last-place showing in 1990. It took the New Yorkers only twenty-four years to become cellar-dwellers again. I hope it's not getting to be a habit.

Horses won't eat it, yet high-priced humans continue to play on it

Astroturf Arrives

JOHN PASTIER

No one could accuse the Astrodome's promoters of thinking small. With typical Texas modesty, in 1965 they labeled the first indoor stadium large enough for baseball and football "the Eighth Wonder of the World."

But they didn't know the half of it. Not until a year after it opened did the Dome attain its real significance. In 1966 it acquired a feature that would make it the most influential stadium of its century, if not of all time, by changing the way that field sports would be played. It did so dramatically, irrevocably, and completely by mistake.

The Astrodome's importance lies not in its cubic footage, roof span, air-conditioning tonnage, or huge skylight, but in its eponymous nylon rug. Astroturf is part of a domino effect of designer-created problems. It's a Band-Aid rather than a solution, creating as many problems as it solves. Nevertheless, it has become a sports industry standard.

The Dome was designed as a greenhouse, with real grass growing under its Plexiglas roof. Its hothouse ecology was carefully planned; its Tifway 419 Bermuda grass was expressly bred to grow indoors. But no one considered the optical qualities of the roof structure and the visual capabilities of the players. Fielders must track a ball of less than three-inch diameter at distances approaching 400 feet and speeds as high as 120 miles per hour. They found that they couldn't reliably follow the ball's flight against the motley backdrop of the Astrodome roof.

The structure for this radical building was conventional if not retrograde. Heavy radial steel ribs formed eight main roof segments that were further divided by a hierarchy of supporting elements for the 4,796 Plexiglas panels. This busy pattern of bright and dark areas created unworkable fielding conditions. Years later, Lowell Reidenbaugh called it a "glaring fault." One story has it that a Dome architect took the field to shag some flies soon after the opening to prove that the fielding backdrop was adequate. After several

futile attempts, he returned empty-handed, saying, "A guy could get killed out there.

Ironically, a more suitable structure had been built seven years before and just 250 miles away. Buckminster Fuller had created a lightweight long-span geodesic dome system at the Union Tank Car repair shops in Baton Rouge, Louisiana. Besides saving money and materials, its uniform pattern of thin struts would almost surely have allowed normal fielding.

But in Houston, it was too late for basic structural rethinking. The skylight was painted gray to lower the brightness and the contrast between panels and structure. Fielders did better on high flies, but the weak light couldn't keep the grass healthy. Again the answer was paint; this time green pigment was sprayed on the brown sod. When the grass finally died, the Astros were ready to play their next season, like the most forlorn of sandlotters, on an all-dirt field.

Before this happened, however, Astropotentate Roy Hofheinz heard of a new nylon "grass" that might serve to carpet his shabby palace floor. The Monsanto chemical company installed roughly 100,000 square feet of its evergreen flooring, and named it in the Dome's honor.

Thus was Astroturf baptized under crisis conditions. In many ways it filled the bill. Being inorganic, it couldn't die. Being dyed, it stayed green. Needing no water, it reduced the dehumidification load on the air conditioning system.

This is not to say that Monsanto's wonder grass produced better baseball through chemistry and ended the Astrodome's woes. Instead it made new ones and spread them throughout the sporting universe. Stadiums that could sustain real grass installed Astroturf or 3M's Tartan Turf to simplify upkeep or to promote the faster game that the speedy surface allowed.

Outdoors, it was a nifty solar heating device, producing

surface temperatures as high as 130 degrees. Not as resilient as grass, it increased fatigue and wear on the legs, joints, and back. Because it didn't give way like grass, it multiplied knee injuries linked to twisting and sudden stops. Bill James observed that "it makes a game painful, which is meant to be played in a kind of controlled joy. Baseball is not football, which is supposed to hurt."

Indoors or out, it turned baseball into a form of pinball, speeding up runners and batted balls alike. A baseball's behavior on turf can be so unreal that players are tricked into thinking that a ball picks up speed on the rug. In the worst cases, turf with a poor subsurface has produced fifteen-foot-high bounces.

Astroturf was an esthetic offense to fans and players brought up on the real thing. Dick Allen declared, "If a horse won't eat it, I don't want to play on it." In his superb short story, "The Thrill of Grass," W.P. Kinsella conjured up a clandestine brotherhood dedicated to resodding turf fields a square foot at a time under cover of night.

Alas, such perceptions carried little weight with sports honchos. Artificial turf became entrenched. Granted, baseball's three fixed-roof domes must use it. Open multipurpose stadiums such as Veterans, Busch, Riverfront, and Three Rivers use it because two-sport schedules are supposedly too tough on real grass. Baseball-only Royals Stadium uses it to minimize games lost due to wet grounds. The Skydome has a working roof that would allow grass to grow, and in theory so does Olympic Stadium, but both use plastic anyway. That's a total of ten. James points out that turf's penetration was effectively halted many years ago, but a purist can argue that we have seven too many rugs in the game. The National League is especially culpable, since only one of its six turf fields is indoors.

Beyond its interior landscaping, the Astrodome had other effects on Houston baseball and football. Its round shape was a poor compromise between proper seating patterns for the two games. Although movable seating sections solved the problem for patrons in the first few rows, most of the seats remained too far from the action of either sport.

For baseball, the Dome's dimensions were large. The painted roof led to dark day games. By keeping temperatures in the low seventies, air conditioning cut down the distance that balls carried. All these factors created the best pitching and worst hitting environment in the major leagues. They reduced scoring by 11 percent and home runs by 38 percent from so-called expected levels over the Dome's first twenty-four seasons.

While one may argue that this led to a subtler brand of play, most fans consider low-offense ballgames boring. The distortions created by the park have made it difficult to appreciate the accomplishments of Astro batters, or to compare them to competitors playing in more normal home parks. Glenn Davis, for example, lost about 14 home runs to the Dome in 1990 alone (his HR production per at bat was 2.3

HOUSTON ASTROS

"Astropotentate" Judge Roy Hofheinz

percent in the Dome and 11.8 percent on the road). And in one seven-year stretch Jose Cruz hit 16 there while hitting 61 on the road. In recent years, the outfield dimensions have been reduced a bit, but the Dome remains a pitcher's park in the extreme, despite an inherent hitters' advantage due to the rug.

After a quarter century, artificial turf is as firmly rooted in baseball as Wrigley Field's ivy. It's clear that ersatz grass has been neither good enough to enrich the sport, nor bad enough to ruin it. It's certainly equally clear that turf fields can be improved.

One step that could be taken easily and quickly is to mandate traditional dirt infields and base paths in all big league parks. The present custom of small dirt sliding pits is mainly a groundskeeper's convenience. Restoring the infield skin would eliminate the baserunner's advantage on nylon. Turf upsets the fine balance between the battery and the base stealer and was a root cause of the dismal tinkering with the balk rule that took place a few years ago. The carpet is to base stealing what the L.A. Coliseum's left field screen was to power hitting.

The other improvements will take some time and faith. The quality of artificial turf and, equally important, that of its resilient subsurface, has advanced over the years. There is no reason to think that further progress can't occur. One fine day, we may have turf that seems more natural to the eye, slows balls down properly, stays as cool as grass, and is as gentle on the knees, legs, and back. Sure, a horse still wouldn't eat it and it would never give off a fresh-mowed aroma, but when was technology ever perfect.

Sandy K.
Is Pitching Today

You better not pout, you better not cry,
You're gonna strike out, I'm tellin' ya why,
Sandy K. is pitching today.

You're gonna look bad and feel even worse,
No matter how much you holler and curse—
Sandy K. is pitching today.

His fastball goes like lightning,
His changeup is a tease.
His curveball starts out toward first base
And then drops across your knees.

You'll swing and you'll miss, just like an old gate
You'll wonder why you brought a bat to the plate—
Sandy K. is pitching today.

– EDDIE GOLD

*Frank Robinson's first season with Baltimore
and his climactic game*

Frank Robinson Inspires Oriole Magic

ROSLYN A. MAZER

The season started on December 9, 1965 when the announcement came after the winter meetings that Robinson was to be traded to the Orioles for pitcher Milt Pappas (13–9).

"I was stunned by the trade, remembered Robinson more than twenty-five years later. The first time you're traded, it hurts you as a person. It hurts you as a player. You think to yourself, 'The team doesn't think I'm good enough'."

He had played ten years for the Cincinnati Reds, earning the 1961 MVP with 37 home runs, a .323 batting average and 124 RBIs. When he learned of the Baltimore trade, though, his memory bank instantly served up an exhibition stop when he was playing for the Reds.

"It was 1957 or 1958, the end of spring training in March, when we made stops for exhibition games on the way back north. We played a game in Baltimore. I had to stay in the black section of town, not in the hotel where the white players stayed. We had two or three black players at the time on the Reds—Brooks Lawrence, George Crowe."

"I told Lawrence I was going to a movie—I was a real moviegoer. Lawrence was smart enough not to go with me. It was pouring down rain. I went up to the ticket window. They wouldn't let me in. . . .I thought about that rainy night when I first heard about the trade to Baltimore."

Happily, Frank's transition to American League ballparks and pitchers was smoother, friendlier.

When the trade was announced, Brooks Robinson now recalls, "some of us were skeptical. We knew what he'd done baseball-wise. But we also knew he'd been arrested with a gun [in a barroom] and had a reputation for being difficult." Some remembered that Robinson had had a knock-down fight with Eddie Mathews in 1960. Frank's left eye was swollen almost completely shut. ("It was my first

fight, first loss, last fight," Robinson said a few years later.)

But from the moment Frank arrived at spring training, "he was the fire that kept us burning," Brooks muses. Perhaps it was a fire ignited by Reds General Manager Bill DeWitt who tried to justify the trade by saying Frank Robinson was "an old thirty." "That remark gnawed at Frank," Brooks says. "We were a breath of fresh air for him—a new team, a new league."

Bill DeWitt

And what an incandescent year it was. Frank's home run tear started in his first at bat in his first appearance in the line-up in a March 15 exhibition game against the Senators, off Buster Narum. He homered off Earl Wilson on Opening Day against the Red Sox, April 12. He hit the first ball ever to leave Memorial Stadium on May 8, off Louis Tiant, a ball that sailed beyond the left field bleachers, landing 451 feet from home plate. Frank hit 49 homers in the regular season, earning one-third of the Triple Crown Award he won that year –

Frank Robinson, an old thirty. Not!

the first since Mickey Mantle won the honor in 1956 – batting .316 and totaling 122 RBIs.

Robinson's defensive talents were crowd pleasers, too. With the Orioles leading 7-5 in the bottom of the ninth with two down, he hurtled into the right field stands on June 21 at Yankee Stadium to make a game-saving catch of a Roy White line drive which would have been a 3-run homer. Frank caught Clete Boyer's line drive to left on August 11 with one out in the ninth inning, ramming the fence and spilling over the barrier, enabling the Orioles to retain their 6-5 lead over the Yanks.

According to Brooks Robinson, "Frank brought out the competitive spirit in all of us, especially the great hitters." Brooks attributes his own sensational first half—he chalked up 81 of his 100 RBIs by July 22—to Frank's example.

Pitcher Dave McNally, now joint owner with his brother of a Ford franchise in his hometown of Billings, Montana, says, "he did it by example. He wasn't a yeller or screamer. We'd be winning a game 10–2 and he would fly into a wall to catch a fly ball. He just gave 100 percent on every play."

Bill DeWitt continued to taunt Robinson in mid-season, assuring sportswriters that the new Orioles would "fade" in July or August. But when Brook's bat cooled in the second half, Frank's offense soared. After trailing both Brooks and first baseman Boog Powell through most of the season, Frank hit 9 homers in one ten-game stretch from July 18 through 29, passed Powell on September 17 with his 107th RBI, then drove in 14 runs in his next five games. His contribution to the Orioles' run production was crucial.

	R	HR	Finished
1965	641	125	3rd, 8 games behind
1966	755	175	1st, 9 games ahead

He was voted MVP, the only player to win the honor in both leagues. (Cincinnati, meanwhile, dropped from fourth to seventh place; Pappas was 12–11.)

The Orioles' storybook season met the cold stares of the oddsmakers after the Orioles clinched the pennant on Sep-

tember 22. The Dodgers were 8–5 favorites to win the World Series, having won in 1959, 1963 and 1965 with manager Walter Alston at the helm. The Dodgers' most elegant arm, Sandy Koufax, had pitched 19 consecutive scoreless innings in Series competition. In 1965, although losing Game Two against the Twins, Koufax won Games Five and Seven, 7–0 and 2–0, striking out 29. Koufax had a 0.38 ERA in his last 24 Series innings.

The Orioles had only one 15-game winner (Palmer, 15–10), only 13 shutouts and the fewest complete games of any pennant winner ever (23). But their pitching staff was underrated, for it made up for what it lacked in experienced starters with a talented bullpen. Especially after starter Steve Barber (10–5) was injured, manager Hank Bauer went to the bullpen whenever he needed to, taking some of the pressure off the youthful starters.

And while the Dodgers had better speed, the Orioles had tremendous sluggers who took the pressure off each other and coerced better pitches, all the while stimulating healthy competition amongst each other. They also had the benefit of what became a legendary scouting report by Jim Russo and Al Bukiski which by some accounts took more than two hours to review at a clubhouse meeting on World Series eve in Los Angeles.

McNally's curveball took a vacation in Game One. Staked to a 3–0 lead after back-to-back home runs by the two Robinsons off Don Drysdale (13–16) in the first inning, McNally (13–6) yielded a home run, a double, five walks and two scorching fly ball outs at Chavez Ravine in 2-1/3 innings, throwing 63 pitches. Moe Drabowsky, who was 5–0 with 4 saves in the regular season, gave "relief" new

Brooks Robinson in the cage.

meaning, striking out 11 in the last 6 2/3 innings, yielding only one hit and two walks. The O's won 5–2.

"I didn't think he had it in him," Frank Robinson now recalls of Drabowsky. "It was one of those magical moments that year."

Twenty year-old Jim Palmer (15-10) pitched a complete game 6-0, 4-hit masterpiece in Game 2 against Sandy Koufax, who was jinxed by a record-tying six errors. It was Palmer's first shutout in 1966. Winging back to Baltimore for game 3, the Orioles' pitching magic continued. Twenty-one year-old Wally Bunker (10-6) pitched a 1-0 complete game, 6-hit shutout. Bunker had been sidelined with injuries in mid-season, hadn't pitched a shutout all year of a complete game since early June. Paul Blair's 430-foot solo home run to center field in the fifth inning combined with masterful defense by Curt Blefary and Luis Aparicio to notch the Orioles' three-quarter mark to the World Championship.

"I was the first one at the ballpark on the morning of Game 4," recalls Brooks Robinson. "It was like a new season. This is what you dreamed about, from the time you sign, to the time you make it to the big leagues and sign your first contract."

McNally and Drysdale, each humiliated in Game One, returned to the mound in Game Four. The Robinson-Drysdale match-up must have stirred up old memories. At a July 1961 game in the L.A. Coliseum (Frank's MVP year with the NL), Drysdale hit Robinson with a pitch following an umpire's warning. Frank went down. "My ball ran in on a righthanded hitter," Drysdale recalls.

NL President Warren Giles fined Drysdale $100 and suspended him for five days. When Drysdale went to pay the fine, he told Giles, "I may be back here again. An umpire or a hitter isn't going to tell me how to pitch."

Scoreless after three, Baltimore's Russ Snyder popped up on the first pitch to start the fourth inning. Next up, Frank Robinson thought he would take the first pitch. But walking up from the on-deck circle and recalling Snyder's popup, Frank says, "I decided I'd be looking for a fastball, from the middle of the plate in." On the first pitch, in a fitting climax to his first season in Baltimore, Robinson belted a waist-high fastball 410 feet into the left field bleachers.

He knew it was gone as soon as it left his bat. So did Drysdale who, when asked twenty-five years later, sadly groaned, "I've heard that sound before.... Actually, it gives me an advantage in the broadcast booth."

The Dodgers got a much-needed emotional lift when Willie Davis, atoning for his three errors in Game Two, brought Boog Powell's sure home run back into the ballpark in the fourth. But the O's turned three critical double-plays in the middle innings. In the eighth, Paul Blair made a breathtaking one-handed catch against the center field fence to rob switch hitter Jim Lefebvre of a homer.

In the bottom of the ninth, McNally a lefthander, faced righthanded Dick Stuart (.242). "Stuart was scary for me. He hit me well when he was with the Red Sox." Stuart made the first out on a called strike. Al Ferrara, another

Don Drysdale delivers

righthander (.270), kept the Dodgers alive by lining a single to center. Nate Oliver came in as a pinch runner, and McNally faced lefthand-hitting Maury Wills (.273), 1-for-13 in the Series, in his final at bat as a Dodger.

At this point not a single Dodger had gotten as far as second base. Wills walked – McNally's second walk in the game, placing the tying run in scoring position. Lefthanded Willie Davis (.284) was now poised to redeem himself offensively and could not have been hungrier: he was 1-for-15 in the Series.

With Drabowsky and Stu Miller warming up, McNally's first pitch was wild, but catcher Andy Etchebarren snared it. On a 1–1 pitch, Davis hit a slow curve to right field, caught by a well-positioned Frank Robinson.

The Dodgers' last hope rested with righthanded Lou Johnson (.272). Harry ("the Cat") Brecheen, the Orioles' pitching coach, trotted to the mound. McNally nodded yes, he was okay, he'd be throwing the curve. Just then, as the runners took their leads, the sun came out from behind a cloud. Home plate umpire John Rice dusted off the plate. Johnson missed the curve ball down and away. Johnson missed another beautiful breaking ball. He swung at McNally's third offering and hit a fly ball deep to center field, where Blair caught the ball to end the Series.

The final score—1–0 on a solo home run—marked only the fourth game in World Series history (368 games in all) to be won by a solo home run. Casey Stengel had done it for the Giants in 1923, Tommy Henrich for the Yankees in 1949. Paul Blair and Frank Robinson earned the third and fourth slots with their back-to-back homers in Games Three and Four.

Young, aggressive starting pitchers, a great bullpen, exceptional sluggers deep into the batting order, flawless defense, a common-sense, intuitive manager, and the ignition and overdrive furnished by Frank Robinson enabled the Orioles to deliver a decisive sweep in their first World Series appearance, vanquishing a great Dodger ballclub.

"The" pitcher for a whole generation

Sandy's Last Hurrah

LYLE SPATZ

There was no more thrilling sight in baseball than that first Koufax fastball.... You go back to Babe Ruth...before you begin to get the idea what Sandy meant to the game
—Jim Murray, *The Los Angeles Times*

In the final year of his career, Sandy Koufax capped an incredible five-year period that was so brilliant it would make him the youngest man ever elected to the Hall of Fame. Bill James in his Historical Abstract ranked him with Lefty Grove as baseball's two greatest pitchers during their peak years.

In 1966 Koufax led the National League in wins, earned run average, strikeouts, innings pitched, and complete games, and tied for the lead in shutouts.

His 27 wins made Sandy the first lefthander in this century to win that many.

His 1.73 earned run average, less than half the NL average of 3.61, was the lowest in the league since Carl Hubbell's 1.66 with the 1933 New York Giants. It was the fifth straight year he had led the league in ERA, breaking a tie with Grove of the Philadelphia Athletics, 1929–1932. The five ERA titles tied Koufax with Grover Alexander for most in the National League.

The performance earned Sandy his third Cy Young Award at a time when no one had ever won it twice, and the award covered both leagues.

Sandy accomplished all this while pitching in excruciating pain from an arthritic elbow. Every time he took the mound it might have been the last time. "The plain fact of the matter is," wrote Jim Murray, "Sandy Koufax shouldn't be throwing a baseball for a living."

As a result of his holdout, Sandy didn't have his first workout until March 31 and worked only two spring games.

Sandy Koufax

Koufax was inconsistent in his first few starts. Yet when he faced San Francisco at home on May 19 his record was 5–1 with five complete games. That night he blanked the Giants, 4–0, allowing three hits and striking out ten. He said after the game that it had been the first time all season that he "felt right".

Five straight complete game victories followed.

But in his next start the Dodgers were beaten on a three-hit shutout by Houston's nineteen-year-old Larry Dierker. Sandy was his idol, said Dierker, "it was undoubtedly the greatest thrill of my life."

Sandy got back on track by winning three consecutive complete games. In the latter two, June 22 in Houston and June 26 in Atlanta, new attendance records were set. It was his first appearance in Atlanta, and lines for standing room began forming at four in the morning. More than 6,000 fans had to be turned away.

In San Francisco, Juan Marichal was also pitching spectacularly, causing writers and fans to wonder if either or both would win 30 games. Of course neither did, and oddly, it was Marichal's teammate, Gaylord Perry, who was first to win 20. Unfortunately, Koufax and Marichal did not face each other that year.

At the All-Star break Sandy's record stood at 15–4. On July 27 he was 17–5. In his next two starts, against Philadelphia and Pittsburgh, he pitched a total of 18 innings, allowed two runs, and had 25 strikeouts (16 against the Phils), but in neither game did he get the win.

On August 9 he lost a 2–1 game to the Braves on a ninth-inning home run by Eddie Mathews. It began to rain during the fourth inning, causing a two-hour delay, but Koufax was kept in the game. The weather had not kept the crowds away, as the attendance record that was set in his previous appearance in Atlanta was broken again.

Koufax was the biggest drawing card in sports.

In 1966 he pitched before 1.5 million fans, an average of 36,000 per game. The National League drew a record 15 million. Thus one out of every ten NL tickets was purchased to see Koufax pitch. He set attendance records at Atlanta and Houston and drew over 50,000 fans eight times.

At about five dollars per fan, including concessions and parking, the Dodgers took in about 7.5 million dollars from Sandy. Yet his salary was an estimated $125,000, and he and teammate Don Drysdale had to stage a double holdout to get that much.

The next year, without Koufax, NL attendance fell by 2 million—almost a million in Los Angeles alone.

Another attendance record fell August 26; pitching in front of the largest crowd in Candlestick Park history, Sandy shut out the Giants, 4–0, for his 21st win.

The pennant race had come down to a three-way battle among the Dodgers, the Giants, and the Pirates.

In a rematch with Dierker September 11, Koufax shut out the Astros, 4–0, to put the Dodgers in first place. Although they struggled the rest of the way, they were never to relinquish the lead that Sandy had given them.

An 11-1 victory against Philadelphia September 20 gave him his 25th win. It made him the first National Leaguer to win that many in two successive seasons since Dizzy Dean in 1934–35, and the first since Alexander to do it three times.

Win number 26 came September 29 against the Cardinals, a four-hit, 2–1 victory in St. Louis. Koufax's 13 strikeouts put him over 300 for the third straight year. Only Rube Waddell and Walter Johnson had ever done that before.

That should have been his last start, but the Dodgers found themselves in Philadelphia on October 2, the last day of the season, needing to win one game of the double-header to prevent a possible playoff with San Francisco.

After they lost the first game and the Giants won their game, there was no doubt about who would pitch game two. Working with only two days rest, Sandy fanned 10 Phillies and beat them, 6–3, to clinch the pennant.

His 317 strikeouts moved him into seventh place on the all-time list.

Sadly, the third strike he threw past Jackie Brandt for his 27th win would be the last pitch he would ever throw in the National League. On November 18 Sandy Koufax, not yet thirty-one, announced his retirement. He was, at the time, the highest paid, most admired player in the game, but he chose to quit "while I can still comb my hair."

SANDY KOUFAX DAY-BY-DAY IN 1966

Date	H/A	Opp.	Score	IP	H	ER	K	Attend	Result
4-13	H	HOU	6–7	3	5	1	2	24,049	-
4-17	H	CHI	5–0	6	5	0	6	32,772	W
4-22		CHI	2–1	9*	6	1	11	4,551	W
4-26	H	STL	4–2	9*	13	2	8	25,121	W
4-30	H	CIN	1–3	9*	6	3	9	44,594	L
5-05		SF	8–9	1.1	4	4	0	26,326	-
5-10		PHI	6–1	9*	6	1	10	14,895	W
5-14		PIT	4–1	9*	7	1	9	11,602	W
5-19	H	SF	4–0	9*	3	0	10	49,409	W
5-23	H	PIT	3–2	9*	8	2	7	24,188	W
5-28	H	NY	7–1	9*	3	0	10	36,389	W
6-01		STL	1–0	9*	7	0	9	36,706	W
6-05		NY	16–3	9*	5	1	8	56,332	W
6-10		SF	6–1	9*	4	1	11	40,048	W
6-14	H	HOU	0–3	8	7	3	6	32,165	L
6-18	H	SF	3–2	9*	4	2	10	54,567	W
6-22		HOU	5–2	9*	9	2	5	50,908	W
6-26		ATL	2–1	9*	7	1	11	51,275	W
7-01	H	STL	0–2	8	5	2	10	38,410	L
7-05	H	CIN	1–0	9*	10	0	8	32,937	W
7-09	H	ATL	2–5	7	6	3	3	47,962	L
7-14		NY	4–2	9*	8	2	11	41,064	W
7-18		PHI	0–4	5	8	3	2	34,755	L
7-23	H	NY	6–2	9*	8	1	7	22,296	W
7-27	H	PHI	2–1	11	4	1	16	44,937	-
8-01		PIT	5–1	7	5	1	9	27,398	-
8-05		HOU	12–1	6	5	1	10	46,555	W
8-09		ATL	1–2	8.1*	4	2	9	52,270	L
8-13	H	CHI	6–1	9*	5	1	11	21,471	W
8-17	H	CIN	1–5	4.1	5	3	4	43,778	L
8-21	H	STL	4–1	9*	6	1	10	33,309	W
8-26		SF	4–0	9*	4	0	7	42,647	W
8-30		NY	4–10	2	4	5	1	50,840	L
9-03		CIN	7–3	6	8	3	4	26,888	W
9-07	H	SF	2–3	7	5	2	6	54,993	-
9-11	H	HOU	4–0	9*	6	0	6	42,978	W
9-16	H	PIT	5–1	9*	5	1	5	54,510	W
9-20	H	PHI	11–1	9*	5	1	6	41,726	W
9-25		CHI	1–2	8*	4	1	5	21,659	L
9-29		STL	2–1	9*	9	4	13	21,615	W
10-2		PHI	6–3	9*	7	2	10	23,215	W
Totals				323	241	62	317	1.5m	27-9

*Complete Game

The Changing of the Guard

The Sandy Koufax-Jim Palmer duel wasn't the first time that future Hall of Famers pitched against each other in a World Series. That first happened in 1884 when Hoss Radbourn beat Tim Keefe.

Nonetheless, Game Two of the 1966 World Series was a symbolic turning point.

I was fortunate enough to attend it. I was a sophomore in college in San Diego at the time and I got an urgent call from my mother that morning that she had just been given two tickets to the game. It was a pleasure to cut classes and speed the 120 miles to Dodger Stadium. We arrived in the second inning.

The Orioles had won a surprisingly easy 5–2 victory in Game One, with first-inning home runs by Frank and Brooks Robinson off Don Drysdale and 11 strikeouts by Baltimore's Moe Drabowsky in relief of Dave McNally. The attitude among the Dodger faithful was that it was a minor delay on the road to certain victory. After all, the best money pitcher of the decade, Sandy Koufax, was going for LA in Game Two.

The Orioles also had good pitching, but it was spread among 11 starters, with Jim Palmer the biggest winner at 15. The bullpen was effective—Baltimore had only 23 complete games. In contrast, the Dodgers used only five starters, with 95 complete games (Koufax had 27 himself).

The Birds were only 29–29 after July 29, largely because of a rash of arm injuries. Steve Barber, who led the starters with a 2.30 ERA, wasn't even activated for the Series.

On the other hand, the Dodgers were in a three-way pennant fight that wasn't decided until the last game of the season, won by Koufax with two days rest. The Orioles were well rested, the Dodgers were not.

THE NEW TOP GUN

Jim Palmer was called "Hollywood" by his teammates because he grew up there watching his hero Sandy Koufax pitch.

Now, aged twenty and having eaten his lucky pregame breakfast of prune pancakes, Jim was about to be one of the youngest men ever to start a World Series game, in his old home town, against his old idol, Koufax.

Only a couple of weeks before, he had clinched the first pennant the O's had ever won, touching off what even manager Hank Bauer, a veteran of many a hard-drinking Yankee team, called the wildest party he'd ever seen. Pitcher Eddie Watt remembered:

"The champagne was up to my ankles, and there was Jim, Coke bottle in his hand, picking his way over the bodies, pushing drunks away. He was looking for a paper cup."

Now Palmer was nervously pacing the locker room before his Series baptism against Koufax, who hadn't given up a run in his last 23 World Series innings. "Well," Jim shrugged, "I'll probably have to pitch a shutout to beat him."

For four innings he matched the Master, each giving only one hit. The Dodgers' Jim Gilliam also fumbled a grounder in the fourth.

Then in the fifth, Sandy's world blew up.

With one on and one out, center fielder Willie Davis dropped Paul Blair's long fly after apparently losing it in the sun. Then Davis lost Andy Etchebarren's short fly, letting one run in. Davis' throw to third was over Junior Gilliam's head, his third error, letting in another run. When Luis Aparicio doubled, a third run came in.

Boos followed Willie to the dugout, where he defiantly tipped his cap to the crowd. Koufax met him in the runway and silently put an arm around his shoulder.

In the sixth, Frank Robinson lifted a long fly to right-center, which Davis and Ron Fairley let fall between them for a three-base hit. Boog Powell singled Frank home. Then Davey Johnson singled and Fairley threw wildly to third for the Dodgers' fifth error of the game.

Koufax loaded the bases with an intentional walk, then got Etchebarren to hit into a DP. It was Sandy's last pitch as a Dodger. He was replaced by relief ace Ron Perranoski to open the seventh.

In the eighth, Perranoski himself made a wild throw to first, the sixth misplay for Los Angeles, letting in another run. It tied the Series record set by the 1906 White Sox, 1909 Pirates, and 1917 White Sox.

In the mean time, Palmer completed a steady four-hitter, becoming the youngest man ever to pitch a World Series shutout. (Waite Hoyt had been 22 when he did it in 1923.)

The papers next morning played up the errors in pictures and text. The *New York Times* forgot to mention Palmer at all until the last two paragraphs of its story. *The Sporting News* also featured the errors and put a small picture of Palmer and Etchebarren on the bottom of its game report over the caption "Baltimore's Baby Battery."

But, as Los Angeles' Lou Johnson pointed out, even without the errors, the Dodgers would have lost, 3–0.

Palmer had thrown 115 pitches, 100 of them fastballs. He told the press that, after watching Drabowsky's 11 strikeouts the day before, "I said I thought the Dodgers couldn't hit a fastball too well."

"Our dope book on Palmer was wrong," said the Dodgers' Maury Wills. "The scouts said his ball had a tendency to rise. It came in straight as a string. He just overpowered us."

Sandy Koufax, the old gunslinger, the fastest draw in the '60s, had been outgunned by the new kid in town, while outside, the Chavez Ravine organist played Taps.

– *DAVID W. SMITH*

The Giants' high-kicker

Marichal the Magnificent

PETER C. BJARKMAN
JOSE DEJESUS, JR.

Juan Antonio Sanchez Marichal was a hard-nosed craftsman with flair, owner of a high-kicking delivery and bulldog competitiveness, the greatest Latin American pitcher in the major leagues.

But he was always misunderstood and under-appreciated by writers and fans. His reputation was that of a hot-blooded renegade "Latino."

And the Dominican Dandy (a nickname in itself part pejorative) was destined to perform in the shadow of more fortune-kissed rivals like Sandy Koufax and Bob Gibson.

Koufax and Marichal dominated an era renowned for great pitching. They were archetypes of the ethnic cultures they represented. Sandy was the brilliant Jewish star, who rose too late and burned out too soon. Marichal was the Latin, considered moody and hot-blooded like Dolf Luque before him and Roberto Clemente alongside him.

In Marichal's first major league game, in 1960—he was only twenty-two—he pitched seven innings of no-hit ball, recording a nine-inning one-hitter against the Phils.

In his first six years his record was:

1960	6–2
1961	13– 10
1962	18 –11 (a pennant-winning year)
1963	25–8
1964	21–8
1965	22 –13

In the last three years he put together Cy Young seasons, only to see Dean Chance beat him once and Koufax twice on the strength of better ERAs. Sandy's Dodgers also won the pennant in '63 and '65, which didn't hurt.

In '65 Marichal also suffered his own darkest moment,

Juan Marichal

when he hit Dodger catcher John Roseboro over the head with a bat.

The two clubs were locked in a tight pennant race when they met in a four-game series in Candlestick Park. San Francisco's hopes were dealt a blow by two extra-inning losses in the first three games. In game four it was Marichal and Koufax head-to-head.

Tension was thick after Marichal knocked down Maury Wills in inning two. Koufax responded with a pitch that sailed over the head of Willie Mays and reached the backstop on the fly.

The Dodgers led, 2–1, in inning three, when Marichal stood in the batter's box. Roseboro reportedly called for a brushback, which the mild Koufax refused to deliver, so Roseboro took matters into his own hands by firing the ball back so close to Marichal's head that it nicked his ear. Angry words were exchanged, Marichal suddenly applied his lumber to Roseboro's skull, and a bench-clearing battle ensured. (Roseboro later admitted in his autobiography his own role.) Once play resumed, Mays struck a three-run homer off the shaken Koufax for a 4–3 Giants victory. But Marichal received an NL record $1,750 fine plus a nine-day suspension. It cost him two pitching starts and a chance to win 24 games. It may also have cost the Giants the pennant—they finished two games behind the Dodgers.

Other Latin hurlers before Marichal had won reputations as hotheads. In 1923 Dolf Luque of Cuba had thrashed Casey Stengel in the opposing dugout. And in the 1950s Puerto Rican Reuben Gomez had brandished a switch-blade at Milwaukee's Joe Adcock.

The incident, one of baseball's ugliest moments, would dog Marichal to the very doors of Cooperstown.

It is also largely forgotten what impact the affair had on the 1966 season.

The following season, '66, the two aces, Koufax and Marichal, were withheld from head-to-head competition, though the Dodgers and Giants battled into September again. Thus Juan lost a chance to redeem himself fully.

Despite a flood of hate mail and boos, Marichal in 1966 shot to a 9–0 start with nine complete games and an 0.59 ERA. Before the summer was out, the villain of the previous season was featured on the cover of *Time* Magazine as "Baseball's Best Righthander."

Marichal three times beat the Dodgers' Don Drysdale, for a 3–0 record against Los Angeles. He had one no-decision when he was taken out in the tenth inning.

On the last day of August, Juan beat the ninth-place Mets, 2–1, to pitch the Giants into a tie for first with Pittsburgh, with Los Angeles three games behind. It was Marichal's 20th victory, just one behind Koufax's 21.

Juan won again September 5, lost five days later, then added another victory on the 14th. However, the Dodgers, with Koufax winning twice, had moved into first, 1.5 games ahead of the Giants and Pirates.

On September 22, with the Giants in third place, four games behind, Juan faced the Pirates and his two Dominican countrymen, Jesus and Matty Alou. Marichal hadn't lost to Pittsburgh in almost two years, but he went into the ninth tied 3–3. The Pirates scored twice in the top of the ninth to take a 5–3 lead. In the bottom of the inning, the Giants smacked two homers to tie it, bringing up Marichal. He swung on the first pitch from Elroy Face (6–6, 18 saves)—"I think it was a slider a little high"—and lined it four rows into the left-field seats to win the game and put the Giants four games behind.

Meanwhile, after four straight wins, Koufax lost to the last-place Cubs, 2–1, on September 26, though Pittsburgh still trailed by 1.5 and San Francisco by 4.

When Juan beat the Braves the next day, the Giants still couldn't move up, as time was running out.

Finally he took the mound against the Pirates on October 2, the next to last day, 3 games behind the Dodgers and 1.5 behind the Pirates. Marichal won the game, 5–4, and the Giants also won the second game to knock Pittsburgh out of second and move into that spot themselves. Ironically, the twin victories virtually clinched the flag for Los Angeles.

Koufax and Marichal had both pitched magnificently down the stretch, Sandy with a 5–1 record and Juan with 6–1. It gave Marichal a final record of 25–6, to Koufax' 27–9.

For the fourth time in four years, Juan Marichal had hurled a Cy Young caliber season only to see someone else snatch the honors. But his victory percentage, .806, was the highest for any man since Lefty Grove in 1931.

Bad timing was Marichal's nemesis. Five times he put together Cy Young years, but each time someone else was hotter.

1963	W–L	ERA	Team
Marichal	25*- 8	2.41	3rd
**Koufax	25*- 5	1.88*	1st
1964			
Marichal	21–8	2.48	4th
**Chance	20*- 9	1.65*	5th
1965			
Marichal	22 –13	2.13	2nd
**Koufax	26*- 8	2.04*	1st
1966			
Marichal	25–6	2.23	2nd
**Koufax	27*- 9	1.73*	1st
1968			
Marichal	26*- 9	2.43	2nd
**Gibson	22–9	1.12*	1st

* Led league

** Cy Young (In 1964 only one Cy Young was given for both leagues.)

The Braves move South

Baseball Comes to the Land of Cotton

DAN LINDER

Atlanta mayor Ivan Allen, Jr., a former president of the Chamber of Commerce, believed that economic growth would create opportunities for the lower class. He built a convention center and cultural center, and Vice-President Hubert Humphrey declared, "If there is a hero on the domestic scene today, it's Ivan Allen of Atlanta."

Allen's next project was to build a major-league stadium and attract a major-league baseball team.

Charles O. Finley, owner of the Kansas City Athletics, realized that Atlanta was the center of the South, almost 500 miles from the nearest major league city. "You build a stadium here, and I guarantee you Atlanta will get a major league franchise," he told Allen. However, Finley was not able to convince fellow American League owners to let him move there.

Meanwhile, Milwaukee Braves owner Bill Bartholmay was looking for a new home. The city of Atlanta was well-known to Milwaukee management from its Cracker farm club in the Southern Association, and the radio and TV market was much larger than those in Milwaukee. Atlanta and Braves officials inevitably reached agreement to move the team in 1965.

Ground was broken for the new stadium, which was completed in a phenomenal fifty-one weeks. The cost was only $18 million. It was built on a downtown site amid thirty-two lanes of traffic and could hold 52,000 baseball fans. Restrooms were designated "Braves" and "Squaws."

The move was delayed a season by a lawsuit in Milwaukee. The Braves did play three 1965 exhibitions in the new stadium. Despite competition from the Masters golf tournament and a major stock car race, over 100,000 fans attended the games. Mayor Allen exclaimed that it was the happiest occasion since General Sherman left town back in 1864.

In one game the Braves started five black players, yet no comments were made by the fans or press.

Many Braves were from the South. Hank Aaron, manager Bobby Bragan, coach Billy Hitchcock, infielder Frank Bolling, and reliever Clay Carroll were from Alabama. Third baseman Eddie Mathews was from Texas, infielder Woody Woodward and pitcher Ken Johnson from Florida, and pitcher Tony Cloninger from North Carolina. Center fielder Mack Jones was from Atlanta, and pitching coach Whitlow Wyatt, who also came from Georgia, was a former manager of the Crackers.

April 12, 1966 marked the debut of major-league baseball in the South. Ironically, it was also the 105th anniversary of the opening shots of the Civil War at Charleston's Fort Sumter. Mayor Allen declared a legal holiday. In a parade down Peachtree Street, the players rode in uniform in open convertibles, along with Clydesdale horses and a jeepful of Playboy Bunnies.

At a black-tie dinner, Dizzy Dean, the guest speaker, was asked who would win the pennant. He responded, "Milwaukee—er, Atlanta."

Bragan, caught up in the euphoria, said, "I wouldn't go back to Milwaukee for all the cheese in Wisconsin."

Fifty thousand fans attended the first regular-season major league game at the new stadium. Pittsburgh pulled it out, 3–2, in thirteen innings, on a home run by Willie Stargell. Atlanta's Tony Cloninger pitched all thirteen innings—remarkable even then—and struck out 12.

On August 9 the brusque, unpopular Bragan was dismissed and replaced by the mild-mannered Hitchcock. Bill's debut that night against Sandy Koufax and the Dodgers drew over 52,000 fans, despite a two-and-a-half-hour rain delay. Pitcher Denny Lemaster, rejoicing at the dismissal of

Bragan, pitched a no-hitter into the eighth inning. Mathews, who had been platooned by Bragan and rarely saw a lefthander that season, hit a pitch into the right-field corner in the ninth, giving the Braves a 2–1 victory.

Hitchcock was popular as a manager. Said Aaron:

"As a manager and a man, Hitchcock was nothing but a gentleman to me. Peculiar that I should even put it that way.... Twenty years ago nobody would have cared what a colored player from Alabama thought about a white manager from Alabama."

What was the impact of the city on the Braves?

In 1965 in Milwaukee the team had played to 500,000 fans and lost $1.5 million. In 1966 in Atlanta it drew 1.6 million fans and made a profit of almost 1 million dollars. The '66 attendance, while impressive, was only sixth best in the league and well below Milwaukee's earlier record high of over 2 million.

What was the team's impact on the city?

The Georgia Institute of Technology estimated expenditures by out-of-town fans in Atlanta to be $6 million. But the prosperity was not translated into fighting poverty. In part because of the recent Nobel Prize for Martin Luther King, Atlanta in the 1960s saw the rise of black power. Inadequate food and housing, plus underemployment, led to increasing racial tension. This cauldron boiled over on September 6, when a riot resulted in seventy-six arrests and one death.

Mayor Allen had said when the new Fulton County Stadium was under construction that, "Major league sports here are a by-product of equal rights. The Negro feels the stadium belongs to him. It's the first new municipal building since the Negro had full citizenship, and some served on the committee that built the stadium."

But there is little evidence of social impact on Atlanta.

Atlanta's 1966 Season

The Milwaukee Braves moved to Atlanta with high hopes of capturing the National League pennant. But their first year in the Peach State ended in disappointment that would mark much of the team's first twenty-five years there.

With irate Milwaukee fans staying away in 1965, the Braves drew half a million and finished fifth with an 86–76 record. In 1966, with 1.6 million Georgians coming through the turnstiles, the Braves were one game worse, 85–77.

Perhaps the move that had the greatest effect on the Braves' future occurred in January, when they selected Tom Seaver of USC for a $40,000 bonus. But since USC had already begun its college schedule, commissioner William D. Eckert nullified the contract. In an unprecedented move, he set up a special draft for any team that was willing to match the Braves' offer. The Mets won out over the Indians and Phillies.

A six-game winning streak in April helped the Braves earn a 13–10 start, but by July 1 Atlanta had its worst record of the season, 34–45. Only a strong September made 1966 respectable.

The long ball was the Braves' favorite weapon in '66, and Atlanta-Fulton County Stadium became known as "the launching pad." There were 201 homers hit there, tops in both leagues. The Braves led the majors with 207.

Henry Aaron decided to alter his batting style: "The ball really flies out of Atlanta Stadium, and when I swing, I'm swinging to put it out of the park. Nothing thrills the fans like a home run, and it's our first season down here, so I'm trying to give them all the thrills I can."

Hank led the league with 44 home runs and 127 RBIs. However, his batting average slid from .318 to .279.

Catcher Joe Torre had the honor of hitting the first Fulton County Stadium home run on opening day. That year he enjoyed his most productive season with 36 home runs and 101 RBIs.

While not remembered for his power, first baseman Felipe Alou boasted 31 homers and finished second in the batting race to his brother, Matty.

Outfielder Mack Jones, despite missing the beginning of the season due to injury, finished with 23 home runs.

Rico Carty became a fan favorite and finished third in the batting race, with 18 homers.

One of the most impressive displays of Braves power came on the road. On July 3 in San Francisco, Tony Cloninger had the best hitting game for a pitcher in major league history. He became the first pitcher to hit two grand slam home runs in a game and drove in nine runs, a record for a pitcher. Cloninger had another two-home run game and finished with the un-pitcher-like record of five home runs, 23 RBI, and one stolen base.

One Brave belted three homers in a game. Gene Oliver, Torre's backup behind the plate, did it July 20 in Atlanta. Ironically, Oliver victimized the same pitchers that Cloninger had—Bob Priddy and Ray Sadecki. Oliver had only five more homers on the season.

The pitching staff didn't have as much to boast about. Cloninger's record dropped from 24–11 in Milwaukee to 14–11 in Atlanta. He had 13 no-decisions.

A bright spot was Clay Carroll. In his first full season he recorded a league high 73 appearances, 8 wins and 11 saves.

Phil Niekro, who would become Atlanta's winningest lifetime pitcher, worked exclusively out of the bullpen in 1966, winning 4 games and earning 2 saves.

Eddie Mathews, the only man to play for the Braves in three cities, had a poor year—.250 with 16 homers. On December 31 he was traded to the Astros.

— RAY MURPHY

Hotfoots, snakes and phone calls

Moe's Mischief

GERALD TOMLINSON

Kansas City, May 27, 1966: The phone rang in the bullpen of the Kansas City A's. Coach Bobby Hofman grabbed the receiver off the wall and heard a voice bark, "Get Krausse hot!"

It was only the second inning, the A's were batting, and their pitcher was in no real trouble. But what was Hofman to do? He figured the call came from Alvin Dark, the A's manager. The voice sounded like Dark's. He told Lew Krausse to start throwing.

The righthander warmed up for only a few moments before the phone rang again. The same voice directed, "Okay, sit him down."

Down sat Krausse.

Across the field in the Baltimore Orioles' pen the Birds were chirping with glee. For it wasn't Alvin Dark at all who had phoned Bobby Hofman. It was the Orioles' righthanded reliever and champion prankster, Moe Drabowsky, who had learned how to make phone contact between the two bullpens.

Yes, Moe was a cutup. Born Myron Walter Drabowsky in Ozanna, Poland, on July 21, 1935, he became "Moe" as a kid when his schoolmates found "Myron" too hard to say. If Moe's nickname had been bestowed later in life, maybe it would have been "Polska" or something like that to match up with two other noted flake nicknames, Herman "Germany" Schaefer and Stanley "Frenchy" Bordagaray.

A 1956 bonus baby off the Trinity College campus in Connecticut, Drabowsky was less the butt of Polish jokes than he was the instigator of them.

Take the time he put a snake in outfielder Lou Johnson's glove. Johnson grabbed his glove to head for the outfield, recoiled when he found it already occupied, threw the glove to the ground in panic, and started kicking it.

Moe Drabowsky

Ah, snakes. Moe couldn't leave them—or his teammates— alone. By the time he got to Baltimore in 1966, he had refined his serpent act. That year he and Oriole pitcher Frank Bertaina bought several live snakes in a pet store. One was a four-foot gopher snake. The other one went

Hank Bauer

They deposited the buddha, knocked on Lau's door, and raced away, leaving Charlie to meet and deal with the huge *objet d'art*.

For all this silliness, Moe Drabowsky was no slouch on the mound. Over a seventeen-year career he won 88 games and lost 105 with a 3.71 ERA. Moe was at his best for Baltimore, 1966 to 1968. In '66 he went 6–0 with a 2.81 ERA. The next two years he posted ERAs of 1.60 and 1.91.

He was at his very best in the first game of the 1966 World Series. Dave McNally started for Baltimore against the L.A. Dodgers, but got into trouble in the third inning. In came Drabowsky, down went the batters—11 of them via strikeouts, six of them in a row. No other relief pitcher had ever recorded 11 strikeouts in a World Series game. Drabowsky and the Orioles won the game, 5–2. The O's won the series 4–0.

The height of his pranksterism came in 1969, the year after he left the Orioles for the Kansas City Royals. The O's won the pennant in '69 and faced the Amazin' Mets in the World Series. For the opening game of the Series, Drabowsky hired a plane to circle Memorial Stadium in Baltimore, trailing a sign that said: "Good Luck Birds. Beware of Moe."

three feet. A while before game time Moe strolled into the visitors' clubhouse at Anaheim Stadium with one of the snakes draped around his neck.

"That's a fake, isn't it, Moe?" outfielder Paul Blair asked.

The big snake raised its head, fixed its beady eyes on Blair, and flicked its tongue.

Blair fled.

He wasn't the first nor would he be the last to flee from Moe's mischief. Oriole manager Hank Bauer learned to live with the constant danger of a Drabo hotfoot; opposing bullpens came to expect finding goldfish in their water cooler, firecrackers dropping in on them from beyond the fence, or the words "Go Birds" painted in bright orange on their dugout.

And then there was the night at the Hotel Grant in Los Angeles. An exhibition of Chinese art graced the lobby—not a good idea with Moe around. He and shortstop Luis Aparicio made off with an enormous golden papier-mache buddha, wrestled it into the elevator, and headed for catcher Charlie Lau's room. Lau ("they pronounced it "Luau") was the designated "Chinaman" for the evening.

Dave McNalley